Shortcuts

for
TEACHING VOCABULARY

by Flora Joy
Illustrated by Pat Harroll

Cover by Janet Skiles

Copyright © Good Apple, 1991

ISBN No. 0-86653-591-8

Printing No. 987654321

Good Apple
1204 Buchanan, Box 299
Carthage, IL 62321-0299

Simon & Schuster Supplementary Education Group

Dedicated to Irene Crowe
The World's Greatest Mom

Hi, folks! You will love this book! It is filled with many fun and challenging vocabulary activities. My favorite is the **Word Twister Cards** found on pages 61-69. I'll bet you can't get even half of them without peeking at the answers on page 142. Try them!

GA1304

TABLE OF CONTENTS

INTRODUCTION

VOCABULARY GAMES AND ACTIVITIES

LISTS, ANSWERS, AND CONTAINERS

GA1304

4

INTRODUCTION

(Note: The design on the back of this page and on pages 4, 12, 14, and 134 are offered as alternatives to the backs of the Worbic deck of playing cards.)

5

GA1304

INTRODUCTION

Without the knowledge of the meanings of words, no subject can be mastered. The understanding of any reading material depends upon the functions, meanings, and interactions of the words in print. Therefore, the skill of vocabulary development must be taught at every grade level and in every subject area.

How should vocabulary be taught? As you consider the answer to this question, look at the following list of fifty words to see how many you know.

Uvulopalatopharyngoplasty, preganglionic, carpospore, psalterium, weltanschauung, chaetognath, flugelhornist, miracidium, ramate, somatomedin, wannigan, dijinni, inegalitarian, rauwolfia, ectocommensal, sphenoidal, ambulacral, daunomycin, impecunious, mydriasis, reive, supinate, xenophobic, echinococcus, kalanchoe, furmity, resinoid, jacquerie, symbiote, azimuth, dugong, jus sanguinis, petidoglycan, riposte, synectics, zygodactylous, glottochronology, lymphogranulomatosis, neume, stomata, peptidoglycan, voticella, bouleversement, extravasate, libeccio, pogonophoran, senryu, vasotocin, coremium, homolecithal.

None of them? Pretend that your assignment is as follows: "Look up these fifty words in the dictionary and write the complete definitions of each one. Include all meanings, etymological facts, and diacritical respellings." What would your response be? What you are feeling might be similar to the feelings of elementary students when they are asked to look up a group of words in the dictionary and write their definitions. This is an activity in which the information can go from fingertip to ballpoint and "bypass" the brain! Such assignments do little other than make learners hate school assignments.

Vocabulary activities do not have to reflect such drudgery. They should be fun, exciting, challenging, and frequently active! The intent of this book is to present a background for teaching vocabulary skills and then offer several ready-to-use activities which have proven successful in hundreds of primary, elementary and middle schools. The main goal for all activities is for students to develop a lifetime appreciation for words and a long-term love of language.

The teaching of vocabulary words should not be haphazard and hit-or-miss. It should be a carefully planned and sometimes structured program designed to acquaint students with a multitude of needed words. In order for this to be a systematic program, the vocabulary subskills should be understood. The following is a discussion of these subskills.

SYNONYMS

Synonyms are words which have similar meanings. They do not always have the **same** meaning, or both words would not be needed in our language. There is always some difference in the shades of meanings of words which are classified as synonyms. A multitude of experiences may be used in the classroom to teach the vocabulary skill of synonyms. The following is one which needs no preparation.

Activity: Sit-Down Synonyms. Divide the entire class into two groups. Have each group line up on opposite sides of the classroom. The first member of one group says a word which has a synonym. The first member of the opposite group repeats the word and gives a synonym for that word. A player who cannot do so sits down and that same word is given to the next person in line. (Yes, one word can seat an entire team!) The player who does respond with an appropriate synonym then gives a new word to the next player on the opposite team. The activity continues until one team has no standing members. The team with members still standing is declared the winner.

A sample wording of this activity is as follows:

First player on Team A: "Give a synonym for the word **cool.**"

First player on Team B: "**Chilly.** Give a synonym for the word **forgetful.**"

GA1304

Second player on Team A: "I can't think of one." (Player sits down.)

Third player on Team A: "I can't think of one either." (Player also takes a seat.)

Fourth player on Team A: "**Absent-minded.** Give a synonym for . . . ." Etc.

Give a synonym for the word **cool.**

Chilly. You give a synonym for the word **forgetful.**

A synonym may be given for any meaning of the word given. When this activity is used frequently, students voluntarily begin using their dictionaries (or parents and friends) to find words which might be used as "seaters" for the other team (always making sure that the word given **does have** a synonym). In the process, they are encountering and learning many new words. Note that this activity may also be used for antonyms, homophones, homographs, and individual word meanings. An adaptation of this activity would be to give each team member two or more opportunities to make a mistake before being seated.

Activity: Euphemisms. The euphemism is a special type of synonym. Although the term might not be used in earlier grades, the concept is still evidenced in the language of all learners. A euphemism (meaning "good sound") is a less offensive or more impressive choice of words than its matter-of-fact counterpart. Rather than saying **false teeth,** the word **dentures** might be used. **Restroom** replaces **toilet, custodian** replaces **janitor,** and **canine control officer** replaces **dogcatcher.** Students can think of "good sounding" words or phrases which they use to describe both their friends and their enemies. If, for example, both a friend and an enemy were perspiring profusely, one might say the friend "glows" but the enemy "stinks." Students may enjoy discussing other euphemisms which they know or have heard.

Activity: Syno-Titles. A player thinks of a popular book title. Instead of saying that title, the player uses synonym replacements for most words (except function words, prepositions, etc.). An example is "The Cat, the Sorceress, and the Closet." The remainder of the players try to guess the original title which is *The Lion, the Witch, and the Wardrobe.* This may extend from book titles to all other types of titles or names of famous things.

Activities in This Book. The following activities are presented in this text for teaching synonyms: **Triple Trouble** (pages 43-60), **Vocabulary Vivacity** (pages 70-78), and **"Said" Is Dead** (page 127). A list of synonyms which may be used for various games and activities is given on page 135.

ANTONYMS

Antonyms are words with opposite or near opposite meanings. Sometimes the concept of "opposite" is difficult for students to grasp, especially younger students. Activities in later sections of this book and below may be used to build this skill.

Activity: Simon Doesn't Say. Select a student to stand at the front of the room. One at a time a seated class member gives him a command. The standing student must do the **opposite** of this command within five seconds. Any student who fails to do so is replaced by the one who gave the command. Much discussion will arise regarding the appropriate wording of such commands. An example is "Whisper your mother's name." The student has two choices—**shouting** his mother's name (instead of whispering it) or whispering his **father's** name (instead of his mother's). Either choice reflects a knowledge of opposites. Many stated commands will have only one choice, and others will have numerous ones. The player needs only to demonstrate his knowledge of **one** antonym, although all may be as linguistically clever as they wish.

This exercise develops quick thinking skills

GA1304

with this phase of vocabulary development.

Activity: Sit-Down Antonyms. This activity is conducted like the Sit-Down Synonyms, explained earlier.

Activity: Anto-Titles. This activity is conducted like Syno-Titles except that antonyms are given for most words instead of synonyms. An example is "Arrived Without the Calm Air" for *Gone with the Wind.*

Activities in This Book. The following activities are presented in this text for teaching antonyms: **Triple Trouble** (pages 43-60), **Vocabulary Vivacity** (pages 70-78), **Vocabulary (Antonym) Cartoons** (pages 79-82), and **Zany Antonyms** (page 128). A list of antonyms which may be used for various games and activities is given on page 138.

HOMOPHONES

Homophones are words which **sound** alike but have different meanings and spellings. The meaning of this term is more easily remembered when each word part is examined. **Homo-** means "the same," and **-phone-** means "sound." (Note that the term **homonym** is often found in vocabulary materials. This concept, however, is much less confusing to learners when it is called either **homophone** or **homograph.**)

Homophones are only misused in **written material.** Therefore, this vocabulary subskill may be closely correlated with spelling. The following activities for teaching homophones require little or no preparation.

Activity: Homophones in Pictures. Select a picture from a magazine, particularly one which has many objects and details. Have students look at this picture and try to identify any item, concept, etc., which has a homophone partner. It is surprising at how many can be identified in a short period of time. Students should offer the spelling of the homophone counterpart.

Activity: Sit-Down Homophones. This activity is conducted like the Sit-Down Synonyms, explained earlier.

A sample wording for use for homophones is as follows:

First player on Team A: "Spell a homophone for **S-E-E.**"

First player on Team B: "**S-E-A.** Spell a homophone for **N-E-E-D.**"

Second player on Team A: "I don't know it." (Player sits down.)

Third player on Team A: "I know it. It's **K-N-E-A-D.** Spell a homophone for . . . ." Etc.

Activities in This Book. The following activities are presented in this text for teaching homophones: **Triple Trouble** (pages 43-60), **Word Twister** (pages 61-69), **Vocabulary Vivacity** (pages 70-78), **Vocabulary (Homophone) Cartoons** (pages 83-86), and **Vocabulary (Homophone) Riddles** (pages 119-122). A list of homophones which may be used for various games and activities is given on pages 139-141.

HOMOGRAPHS

Homographs are words which are spelled alike but which have different meanings and occasionally different pronunciations. (**Homo-** means "the same," and **-graph-** means "written.") The word **run,** for example, has approximately 150 meanings listed in *Webster's Ninth New Collegiate Dictionary.* This is a very important subskill in language development because of the many possibilities of misinterpreting meaning if only one definition of a word is known. The following are some exercises which may be used to build this skill.

Activity: Sit-Down Homographs. This activity is conducted like the Sit-Down Synonyms, explained earlier.

A sample wording for use with homographs is as follows:

First player on Team A: "We had **turkey** for Thanksgiving dinner. Use the word **turkey** in a sentence which shows a different meaning of the word."

First player on Team B: "You are a **turkey!** (Ho! Ho!) My uncle had a **heart** attack. Use the word **heart** in a sentence which shows a different meaning of the word." Etc.

Activities in This Book. The following activities are presented in this text for teaching homographs: **Homograph Grins** (pages 23-42), **Triple Trouble** (pages 43-60), **Word Twister** (pages 61-69), **Vocabulary Vivacity** (pages 70-78), and **Vocabulary (Homograph) Cartoons** (pages 87-90).

STRUCTURAL ANALYSIS

Structural analysis skills involve the breaking down of the word into its separable parts: roots, prefixes, suffixes, or other syllables. Knowledge of these parts may aid in determining the meaning of many individual words. A variety of activities may be used to build the vocabulary subskill of structural analysis. The following are some which require little or no preparation.

Activity: Compound Competition. Divide the entire class into two groups. Have each group line up on opposite sides of the classroom. The first member of one group says a word which is a compound word. The first member of the opposite group takes the last word of the stated compound and uses it as the first part of **a new compound word.** A player who cannot do so sits down and the next player gives a new compound word. This continues until an entire team is seated. The team with remaining standing winners is declared the winner. Sample wording for this activity is as follows:

First player on Team A: "Doorbell."
First player on Team B: "Bellboy."
Second player on Team A: "Boyfriend."
Second player on Team B: "Friendship."
Third player on Team A: "Shipyard."
Third player on Team B: "Yardstick."
Fourth player on Team A: "Stickshift."
Instructor*: "**Stick shift** is two separate words. Can you think of another one?"
Same player: "Stickpin."
Fourth player on Team B: "Pineapple."

Instructor: "Sorry, but the first part of this is **pine** instead of **pin.** Can you think of another one?"
Same Player: "Pincushion."
Fifth player on Team A: "I can't think of a compound word beginning with **cushion.**" (Player sits down.)
Sixth player on Team A: (Starts with **new** compound word.) "Gentlemen."
Fifth player on Team B: "Menu."
Instructor:* "Sorry, but that is not a compound word." (Player sits down. There are no compound words which begin with **men.**)

The game continues until one team is completely seated. Note that students may search and discover words (like **pincushion** and **gentlemen**) which are sure "seaters" for one person on the opposite team. This aids in the learning and understanding of many new words.

*No instructor can automatically know every word in the English language. It is suggested that one or two students be declared "neutral" to look up questionable words which are given as responses by players. Even the best of linguists do not automatically know whether words are compound, hyphenated, or simply two separate words. When either of the latter is given, the player has another opportunity to think of an appropriate compound word. No time limits are generally imposed with this activity.

Activities in This Book. The following activities are presented in this text for teaching structural analysis skills: **Triple Trouble** (pages 43-60), **Vocabulary Vivacity** (pages 70-78), **Worbic** (pages 99-118), and **Who's Afraid of Phobophobiacs?** (page 129).

INDIVIDUAL WORD MEANINGS

Many words simply must be learned as individual words. These are words which cannot be broken down and analyzed according to their component parts or which are not easily learned

10

GA1304

in connection with synonyms or antonyms. There are many activities for learning such words.

Activity: Sit-Down Words. This activity is conducted like the Sit-Down Synonyms, explained earlier. A sample wording for use with individual word meanings is as follows:

First player on Team A: "Use the word **flexible** in a sentence."

First player on Team B: "Our plans for a classroom field trip must be **flexible** because of the possible bad weather. Use the word **torment** in a sentence.

Second player on Team A: "I like to **torment** my little brother. Use the word **subject** in a sentence.

Second player on Team B: "This is a **subject.**"

Interrupting player on Team A: "No. That sentence does not show that you know any meaning of the word **subject.** Use another sentence which will **prove** that you know what it means!"

Second player on Team B: "The **subject** of a sentence is a noun or pronoun. Use the word **taximeter** in a sentence.

Third player on Team A: "I don't know what it means, and I don't think you do either. Before I sit down, **you** must use it in a sentence!"

Second player on Team B: "Easy enough. The cabdriver pointed to the **taximeter** to show me that I owed him $8.50." (Player 3 on Team A is seated and the next player gives a new word to be used. Note that before a word can "seat" a player on the opposing team, the word-giver must demonstrate knowledge of its meaning.) The game continues until a team is seated.

Activities in This Book. Individual word meanings may be taught in correlation with other vocabulary subskills. The following activities are presented in this text for teaching individual word meanings: **Homograph Grins** (pages 23-42), **Triple Trouble** (pages 43-60), **Word Twister** (pages 61-69), **Vocabulary Vivacity** (pages 70-78), **Vocabulary Cartoons**

(pages 79-98), **Worbic** (pages 99-118), **Vocabulary Riddles** (pages 119-126), **"Said" Is Dead** (page 127), **Zany Antonyms** (page 128), **Phobophobiacs** (page 129), **Eponyms** (page 130), and **Those Crazy Idioms** (pages 131-132).

SPECIAL PHRASE MEANINGS

Sometimes words are grouped together in a manner which causes the meanings of each separate word to change. Such special phrases have meaning **as a phrase only.** Most proverbs or expressions which are used daily, such as "He's a shady character," cannot be interpreted simply by determining the meaning of each separate word. A variety of exercises may be used for learning these special phrase meanings.

Activities in This Book. The following activities are presented in this text for teaching special phrase meanings: **Triple Trouble** (pages 43-60), **Vocabulary Vivacity** (pages 70-78), **Vocabulary (Expressions) Cartoons** (pages 93-98), **Vocabulary (Expressions) Riddles** (pages 123-126), and **Those Crazy Idioms** (pages 131-132).

OTHER VOCABULARY SUBSKILLS

The above seven groupings of vocabulary subskills certainly do not cover the complete vocabulary spectrum, but they are adequate for teaching vocabulary in elementary and middle grades. Other categories of studying words can prove to be interesting and challenging. Page 130, entitled **Eponyms,** provides one such additional skill area. The point to remember with all vocabulary study is that students should **enjoy** learning new words! (Remember how **you** felt with the thoughts of the task of looking up fifty unknown words listed on page 7?) When the material becomes a drudgery, it should be replaced with something more exciting!

GA1304

GA1304

VOCABULARY GAMES AND ACTIVITIES

(Note: The design on the back of this page and on pages 4, 6, 12, and 134 are offered as alternatives to the backs of the Worbic deck of playing cards.)

14

GA1304

ACTIVITY EXPLANATIONS

The remainder of this text offers a variety of easy-to-prepare activities which will assist in the development of the previously explained vocabulary subskills. The directions for using each separate activity are explained in detail. Following these explanations, the corresponding pages of reproducible materials are provided.

Preparation of Activities

All of the following activity pages may be photocopied for use with individuals or groups. The pages may be copied onto regular or heavy paper and subsequently protected with laminating film or clear self-adhesive paper such as Con-Tact. Those pages containing smaller cards may then be cut into separate pieces. Answers may be written or typed on the backs of the cards for those activities needing them. Two activities (Triple Trouble and Vocabulary Cartoons) have answers which automatically appear on the backs of the cards. The pages for that exercise may be carefully cut from this book rather than photocopied (if desired). Additionally, the Worbic deck may be prepared in the same fashion because of the decorative playing-card pattern appearing on the backs of the cards.

Explanation for HOMOGRAPH GRINS

Pages 23-42 provide twenty full-page task cards for teaching the vocabulary/comprehension subskill of interpreting homographs. These pages offer a variety of formats for the learners, such as crossword puzzles, word search puzzles, cartoons and riddles. The answers for these tasks appear upside down in small type at the bottom of each page. Each card contains items which are relatively easy in addition to those which are considered challenging. Because of the provided answers, learners are not placed in an embarrassing position of revealing any linguistic ignorance.

Explanation for TRIPLE TROUBLE

Pages 43-60 provide 135 small cards (gradually progressing in difficulty) for all vocabulary subskills. Each card contains the following:

1. A topic (subject area or subskill)
2. A question and/or an explanation of this skill
3. Three items to be answered by the players
4. The answers (on the backs of the cards)

TRIPLE TROUBLE CARD 11
WORDS ENDING WITH -RN: The following describes words which end with **-rn.** What is each word?

A vegetable

Thick thread

To grieve

These cards may be used in a variety of ways. The following is an explanation of one suggested activity:

1. Divide all players into groups of three.
2. Give each group a stack of cards relating to their interests and ability level. These cards should be placed inside an envelope or covered so that **no writing** can be previously viewed by any player.
3. One player, designated as the **leader,** selects a card and holds it in a fashion that no remaining player can view any of the printed words on either side of the card. The leader reads the category and question/explanation **aloud** to the two remaining players, then places the card on a desktop for them to view the three items in large type. Immediately the leader begins counting slowly to fifteen.

GA1304

4. During these fifteen seconds (or other designated time period) the two players respond to the three items printed in large type on the card. It is possible for one player to answer all three, for one player to answer one and the other

player to answer two, or for one or more items to remain unanswered. At the end of the fifteen seconds, **one point** is given to the player(s) who **first** provided appropriate answer(s). Up to three points may be given for each card unless an answer is uttered by two players at the *exact same instance,* in which case **both** players are credited with having a right answer. For any unanswered items during the allotted time period, the points are given to the leader. The leader is responsible for calculating the time and for determining the accuracy of the answers given by the two players. The leader may privately glance at the answers **prior to** reading the question in order to know if those responding have provided correct answers.

5. The scores are recorded for that card. The points will accumulate throughout the playing period.

6. For the **second card** a different student is

the leader, and the two remaining students are the players. The position of leader will rotate for each new card.

7. The winner is the student with the highest score at the end of the playing period.

Several adaptations of the above suggested procedure may occur because of the learning styles and interests of the players. Also, many additional cards may be prepared for the continuation of this activity.

Explanation of WORD TWISTER

Pages 61-69 provide 81 small cards for fun with vocabulary. The skills involve both homophones, homographs, and possible mispronunciations of similar sounding words.

(Answer: illegal)

Learners are asked to examine the pictures of the words which have been "twisted" because of a misunderstanding. The answers (provided on page 142) may be written or typed onto the backs of photocopies of the provided pages.

Students may be encouraged to prepare their own versions of Word Twister cards to add to this collection.

GA1304

Explanation of VOCABULARY VIVACITY

Pages 70-78 provide 144 small cards which give learners experiences with many different vocabulary subskills. The following is one suggested procedure for the activity:

1. The small prepared cards are placed in several envelopes, each containing a minimum of four cards. All players may be divided into teams of two. One of these players on each team is designated as the **clue giver,** the other as the **clue receiver.**

2. When the timekeeper gives a signal, all clue givers randomly (without looking) select **one** card from their envelopes. They make sure that at no time can the partners see the printed words on the selected card. They announce the category (found at the top of each card) to their partners and begin giving clues (aloud) for the words which follow in large type. The goal is to prompt the partners to say (aloud) as many of the eight printed items as possible within the designated time limits (usually one minute). Clue givers do not have to proceed in the order of the items on the card. It is wise to give clues for the most familiar items first, then proceed to the harder ones.

The category is words rhyming with **BE.** A body of water.

Sea

It unlocks a door.

Key

It's an insect.

Bee

No, a smaller one that bites dogs.

Oh, a flea.

Vocabulary Vivacity
Words Rhyming with BE

sea
key
flea
ski
agree
honeybee
chimpanzee
referee

3. Regarding the giving of the clues, all players must be previously informed that the clue givers **must not say any part of the words in large type.** For example, if the word is *birthday,* the clue may not contain the words *birth* or *day.* Clues such as "the day of your birth," "the day you were born," or "the celebration of your birth" would not be acceptable. In case of such misclues, the specific item should be dropped and no point could be recorded. Gestures and other nonverbal clues **are** acceptable. Clue givers are encouraged to expand their hints into phrases and sentences, thus not restricting them to the "one word, then wait" style. Frequent classroom discussions may occur before and after the playing time in order to allow all players to hear a variety of possible clues from other class members.

4. At the end of the time limit, the timekeeper calls time. Any word uttered after this signal cannot count as a response. Both players on the team now look at the card and count the number of items which were guessed by the clue receiver. This number is recorded for **both** members of the team.

5. The positions of the team members now switch. The one who was previously the clue giver is now the clue receiver, and vice versa. Step 2 is now repeated. The points accumulate for each card. The game continues for as many rounds as desired. The winner is the **team** with the highest number of accumulated points.

There are many adaptations to the above procedure. One successful modification is for the **entire class** to be divided into **two** groups. Two members from one group are called to the front and handed a card. They are given a few seconds to glance at the items; then the timekeeper gives a signal. The category is announced and **both volunteers** give clues to their half of the classroom. Anyone in that half may say the answers aloud. As soon as a correct response is heard, the clue givers proceed to a new item. There is no penalty for inappropriate guesses. Should a member of the opposite team

GA1304

inadvertently utter a correct response aloud, it **counts**—not for their own team, but for the team giving the clues. (This seems to take care of those who tend to speak out of turn.) One point is given for each response voiced within the time limits. The activity rotates from one side of the room to the other as long as desired. The winning half of the classroom is the one having the higher number of points.

Many other modifications of this activity may be used. Also, instructors or players may prepare additional rounds of cards for this exercise.

Explanation of
VOCABULARY CARTOONS

Pages 79-98 provide thirty cartoon cards which give students humorous experiences as they learn more about antonyms, homophones, homographs, expressions, and individual word meanings. The answers for these cartoons appear on the backs of the cartoon pages.

Following the use of these cartoons, students should be encouraged to prepare additional ones which could demonstrate one of these vocabulary subskills. The cartoons from the daily newspapers should be brought to class regularly to use for the identification (and preparation) of any cartoons which may be used to teach vocabulary skills.

Explanation of
WORBIC

Pages 99-118 provide a deck of ninety playing cards which learners may use to build the vocabulary subskills of structural analysis. Twenty-seven of these are prefix cards, eighteen are suffix cards, thirty-five are root cards, and ten are "wild" cards. The wild cards may be used for any prefix, root, or suffix in the English language. Many of the frequently used prefixes and suffixes are repeated because of their frequent occurrence in our language. These cards appear in this book with a playing card design on the backs. These sheets may be carefully cut from the book and laminated for immediate use. Should a different design for the card backs be preferred, one of the alternate page designs (pages 4, 6, 12, 14, and 134) may be used.

The goal of these playing cards is for learners to have experiences with **prefixes, roots, and suffixes** as these word forms combine to make polysyllabic words. All activities suggested below incorporate the concept of the placing of these cards in order to make words. Each prefix card contains a large half-oval with the rounded part to the left. The open part of this oval has dotted lines to indicate that something needs to be added before there is a complete word.

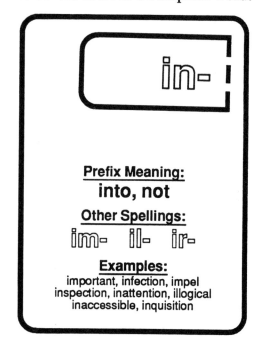

The root cards are left open at both right and left ends, thus indicating that other word parts may be added at either place.

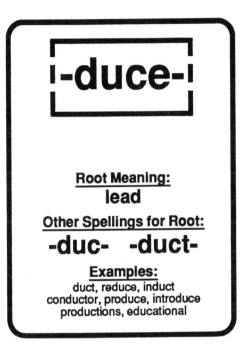

The suffix cards are half-ovals which are the mirror images of those for prefixes.

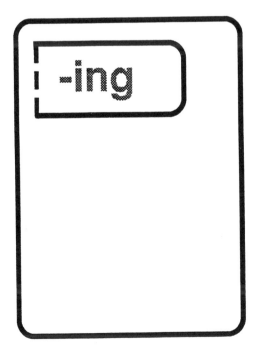

The following shows one way these cards are placed together to form a word:

In addition to the information found in large type at the top of each card, the prefix and root cards offer the **meanings** of the word form on the card. All cards offer alternate spellings, when appropriate. For example, the prefix **con-** card offers alternate spellings of **co-, com-** and **col-.** All except the suffix cards offer eight examples of words containing that word form.

Many activities may occur with this deck of cards. The following are some suggestions:

Activity 1 (For 2-20 players): Remove the wild cards and shuffle the remaining deck. Have the learners gather close. Quickly show the top card to all players. The first player who says a word containing that word form receives the card. The game continues until the complete deck has been distributed among the players. The winner is the one with the most cards.

Activity 2 (For 2-6 players): Remove both the wild cards and the repeated cards, and shuffle the remainder of the deck. Show the top card to the first player. That player has one minute to name as many words having that word form as possible. The player receives one point for each acceptable word. The second player does likewise. The activity continues in this manner until each player has had four turns. The winner is the one with the highest number of points. (Players will soon ask if inflected forms of the words will count as separate words. Certainly so! After all, that is the point of the game.)

Activity 3 (For any number of players): Proceed as above, only have the players **write** the words rather than say them aloud. All players would be writing at the same time in response to the same card.

Activity 4 (For 2-6 players): Place all cards facedown on a tabletop. The first player turns

over two cards. If these two cards can form a word, that player keeps both cards if he/she can spell the word aloud and use it in a sentence. If the two cards do not form a word, the player turns them back over and leaves them in the same position on the table. Other players attempt to remember the items on the previously overturned cards. The next player turns over two cards and continues in the same manner until about ten cards remain on the table. The winner is the one with the highest number of cards.

Activity 5 (For 2-6 players): The dealer deals fifteen cards to each player. Players try to form words with these cards, using each card only one time. The points given are dependent upon the word length.

A one-card word (such as **serve**) receives **five points.**

GA1304

A two-card word (such as **in/spect**) receives **twenty points.**

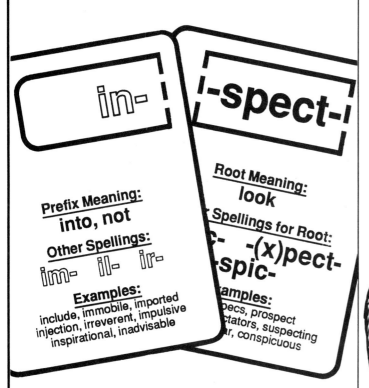

A three-card word (such as **con/tain/s**) receives **fifty points.**

A four-card word (such as **pre/scrip/tion/s**) receives **one hundred points.**

> I have a four-card word! It is **infections**. That is one hundred points. I have three three-card words, **tractors**, **pressuring**, and **imported**, for fifty points each, and **receive** for twenty points. My total is 270. Surely I win!

A five-card word (such as **un/ob/ject/-ion/able** or **in/spir/ation/al/s** receives **two hundred points.**

> Hold it up there, Buster! No way! I have a five-card word, **unimportantly**. That's two hundred points. I also have **infect**, **question**, and **respect**. That's twenty each for sixty more points. I have **claim** for five points and three discards for no credit. That's 265 points. Oops! I guess you win after all!

The player with the highest number of points is declared the winner. That winner must **spell** each word correctly and use it in a sentence which reflects knowledge of the meaning.

A multitude of additional uses may be found for this deck of cards. For all activities, many separate language skills may be taught. The alternate spellings (provided on most cards) should be frequently discussed. For example, if a player is holding the cards **con-** and **-miss-** while trying to form a word, he might overlook the word **commit** if the alternate spellings of both word forms have been ignored. **Thousands of words** may be formed with these cards when all of these spelling alternatives are considered. This is a very important step in building the vocabularies of all learners!

Explanation of VOCABULARY RIDDLES

Pages 119-126 provide 192 riddle cards which may be used to build the vocabulary subskills of homophones or expressions. Learners may have a delightful time answering these and additionally thinking of other riddles to add to this collection.

Explanation of "SAID" IS DEAD: A SYNONYM ACTIVITY

Page 127 is an activity for helping learners substitute synonyms for the overused **said.** Bordering the page are dozens of words in small type which are synonyms for **said** (in case they can't think of any). There are no "right" activities for this page. Students are encouraged to think through the best choice for each situation in the story. Several volunteers may read the passage with their choices of synonyms. They should then be encouraged to use these substitutions in future speaking and writing.

THE ADDED CHALLENGE: ACTIVITIES FOR THE SUPER BRIGHT

Explanation of ZANY ANTONYMS

Page 128 is a fun exercise with antonyms. It makes fun of our language in a tongue-in-cheek manner. Bordering this page are pairs of antonyms which students may examine if they wish. Answers for this activity are given on page 142.

Explanation of WHO'S AFRAID OF PHOBOPHOBIACS?

Page 129 gives an exercise in trying to determine what a word means without looking it up in the dictionary. If students examine the beginning part of the word, then study the accompanying pictures, they should be able to make appropriate matches. Answers for this activity are provided on page 142. *Thanks to Dura Dittmar for providing the illustrations for this exercise.*

Explanation of EPONYMS FOR VOCABULARY FUN

Page 130 provides an activity for the little-known eponyms. Answers for this exercise are given on page 142.

Explanation of THOSE CRAZY IDIOMS

Pages 131-132 offer eleven cartoon experiences concerning the meanings and interpretations of idioms. Answers for these are given on page 142.

GA1304

Homograph Grins

Topic: A **DRAW**ing Lesson

One meaning of the word **draw** is "to sketch or trace." If this is the **only** meaning known for this word, a listener might misinterpret many expressions using the word **draw**. Below are some "drawings" of some possible confusions. Can you determine what was heard in each case? (Words with many different meanings are called **homographs.** How many other expressions using the word **draw** do you know?)

Answers: *1. Draw the drapes. 2. Draw flies. 3. Draw attention. 4. Draw a gun. 5. Draw up a will. 6. Draw straws. 7. Draw a card. 8. Draw a blank. 9. Draw names. 10. Draw the line. 11. Draw a crowd. 12. Draw conclusions.*

23

GA1304

Homograph Grins

Topic: Time for a CHANGE

Many words have more than one meaning even though their spelling is not altered when the meaning is modified. Such words are frequently called **homographs.** Sometimes humorous situations may occur when only one meaning of a word is known. Examine the following situations and determine as many meanings of the word **change** as you can. Have fun!

Answers: Some meanings of change are as follows:
A fresh article of clothing (as in diapers);
Money, generally in coins or small denominations;
To switch, as in one set of clothes with another;
To put on different clothes.
How many more meanings of the word change do you know!

24

GA1304

Homograph Grins

Topic: Body Language

Homograph Grins activities are intended to aid in developing the vocabulary/comprehension skill of interpreting homographs. Words which are **spelled** the same but have different **meanings** are often called **homographs.** Because of these identical spellings but different meanings (and sometimes different pronunciations), often the reader or listener miscommunicates. The following activities help develop an awareness of the multiple meanings of selected words. Work them and have fun!

A. HOMOGRAPH RIDDLES. Read and answer the following riddles. What is the homograph in each one?

1. What do you call a sunburn on your stomach?
2. Why is your heart like a policeman?
3. Why did the man always have his arm in a sling?
4. What do you tell someone who has water on the knee?
5. What happened when the streaker was taken to court?

B. HOMOGRAPH VISIONS. A "homograph vision" is a drawing of a *misunderstood* homograph. See if you can determine what word or expression was originally said to create the inappropriate "vision" shown at the right.

I used to have a set of wooden teeth!

That's nothing! I think my grandmother used to have a cedar chest!

C. HOMOGRAPH CARTOONS. Can you determine the two different meanings of the homograph in the cartoon at the left?

Answers: A. 1. Pot roast (Pot) 2. They both have a regular beat. (Beat) 3. Because he got all the breaks (Breaks) 4. Wear pumps. (Pumps) 5. They were not able to pin anything on him. Also, he refused to take the wrap. (Pin and wrap) B. A kneecap C. The homograph is chest.

GA1304

Homograph Grins

Topic: Tooth and Nail

Homograph Grins activities are intended to aid in developing the vocabulary/comprehension skill of interpreting homographs. Words which are **spelled** the same but have different **meanings** are often called **homographs**. Because of these identical spellings but different meanings (and sometimes different pronunciations), often the reader or listener miscommunicates. The following activities help develop an awareness of the multiple meanings of selected words. Work them and have fun!

A. HOMOGRAPH RIDDLES. Read and answer the following riddles. What is the homograph in each one?
1. Why didn't the old woman use toothpaste?
2. Why do dentists get fat?
3. What has teeth but cannot eat?
4. What kind of teeth can you buy with a dollar?
5. What is the highest rank a dentist can achieve in the army?

B. HOMOGRAPH VISIONS. A "homograph vision" is a drawing of a *misunderstood* homograph. See if you can determine what word or expression was originally said to create the inappropriate "vision" shown at the right.

C. HOMOGRAPH CARTOONS. Can you determine the two different meanings of the homograph in the cartoon below?

Answers: A. 1. Her teeth weren't loose. (Paste) 2. Almost everything they touch is filling. (Filling) 3. A comb (Teeth) 4. Buck teeth (Buck) 5. A drill sergeant (Drill) **B.** An eyetooth (An eyetooth is a canine tooth of the upper jaw.) **C.** The homograph is file. One meaning is to place in an order among other records. Another meaning is to rub or smooth away.

GA1304

Homograph Grins

Topic: Monsters and Ghosts

Homograph Grins activities are intended to aid in developing the vocabulary/comprehension skill of interpreting homographs. Words which are **spelled** the same but have different **meanings** are often called **homographs.** Because of these identical spellings but different meanings (and sometimes different pronunciations), often the reader or listener miscommunicates. The following activities help develop an awareness of the multiple meanings of selected words. Work them and have fun!

A. HOMOGRAPH RIDDLES. Read and answer the following riddles. What is the homograph in each one?

1. How can you get inside a locked cemetery at night?
2. Why did Dracula go to the orthodontist?
3. What is a monster's favorite ball game?
4. Why didn't the skeleton tell the witch how ugly she was?
5. What do you do with blue ghosts?

B. HOMOGRAPH VISIONS. A "homograph vision" is a drawing of a *misunderstood* homograph. See if you can determine what word or expression was originally said to create this inappropriate "vision" shown above at the right.

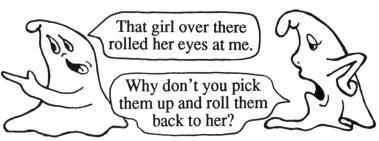

That girl over there rolled her eyes at me.

Why don't you pick them up and roll them back to her?

C. HOMOGRAPH CARTOONS. Can you determine the two different meanings of the homograph in the cartoon at the left?

Answers: A. 1. With a skeleton key (Skeleton) 2. To improve his bite (Bite) 3. A doubleheader (Head) 4. He didn't have the heart to. (Heart) 5. Cheer them up. (Blue) B. The word was ghostwriter. The homograph is ghost. One meaning of ghost is a spirit or soul thought to have left the body of a dead person. Another meaning (as in ghostwriter) is to write for someone else who will be the presumed author. (Political speeches are often prepared by ghostwriters.) C. The homograph is roll. One meaning is to impel forward by causing to turn over and over on a surface. Another is to shift a gaze continually.

GA1304

Homograph Grins

Topic: Footnotes

Homograph Grins activities are intended to aid in developing the vocabulary/comprehension skill of interpreting homographs. Words which are **spelled** the same but have different **meanings** are often called **homographs.** Because of these identical spellings but different meanings (and sometimes different pronunciations), often the reader or listener miscommunicates. The following activities help develop an awareness of the multiple meanings of selected words. Work them and have fun!

A. HOMOGRAPH RIDDLES. Read and answer the following riddles. What is the homograph in each one?
1. What kind of problem does a five-foot man have?
2. Why isn't your hand twelve inches long?
3. What has a head and a foot but cannot think or walk?
4. What did one toe say to the other toes?
5. What has a foot on each side and one in the middle?

B. HOMOGRAPH VISIONS. A "homograph vision" is a drawing of a *misunderstood* homograph. See if you can determine what word or expression was originally said to create this inappropriate "vision" shown at the right.

C. HOMOGRAPH CARTOONS. Can you determine the two different meanings of the homograph in the cartoon shown at the right?

He who puts his foot in his mouth sometimes ends up with a sock in his jaw.

Answers: **A.** 1. *He needs two and one half pairs of shoes. (Foot)* 2. *Then it would be a foot. (Foot)* 3. *A hill (Head and foot)* 4. *"There's a heel following us." (Heel)* 5. *A yardstick (Foot)* **B.** *"A footprint"* **C.** *"Foot in mouth" and "sock in jaw" are two expressions. The homographs are foot and mouth.*

GA1304

Homograph Grins

Topic: "Cross" Words

Homograph Grins activities are intended to aid in developing the vocabulary/comprehension skill of interpreting homographs. Words which are **spelled** the same but have different **meanings** are often called **homographs.** Because of these identical spellings but different meanings (and sometimes different pronunciations), often the reader or listener miscommunicates. The following activities help develop an awareness of the multiple meanings of selected words. Work them and have fun!

What do you get when you cross
1. a computer with a rubber band?

2. an ocean with a thief?

3. a California telegraph operator with an Arizona telephone operator?

4. an earthquake with a forest fire?

5. a stereo with a refrigerator?

6. poison ivy with a four-leaf clover?

7. Why did the hen cross the street?

8. When is a person not a person?

9. When are the roads unpleasant?

10. Why was the farmer cross?

11. Why did Lee find words that meant "angry"?

12. Why did the farmer cross his chickens with his parrot?

Answers: 1. A gadget that makes snap decisions 2. A crime wave 3. A western union 4. Shake and bake 5. Very cool music 6. A rash of good luck 7. To see a man lay bricks 8. When he is a little cross 9. When they are crossroads 10. Because someone stepped on his corn 11. To make a crossword puzzle 12. To get a bird that would tell him when she laid eggs.

GA1304

Homograph Grins

Topic: "All Ears"

Homograph Grins activities are intended to aid in developing the vocabulary/comprehension skill of interpreting homographs. Words which are **spelled** the same but have different **meanings** are often called **homographs.** Because of these identical spellings but different meanings (and sometimes different pronunciations), often the reader or listener miscommunicates. The following activities help develop an awareness of the multiple meanings of selected words. Work them and have fun!

A. HOMOGRAPH VISIONS. A "homograph vision" is a drawing of a *misunderstood* homograph. See if you can determine what word or expression was originally said to create the following "visions."

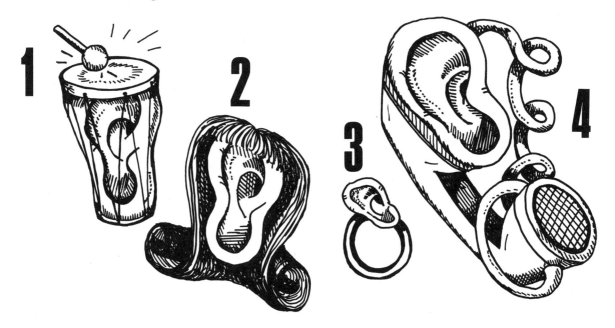

B. HOMOGRAPH CARTOONS. Can you determine the two different meanings of the homograph in the cartoon at the right?

I have always wondered why Van Gogh didn't become a musician.

Maybe he just didn't have the ear for it!

Answers: A. 1. Eardrum 2. Earwig 3. Earring 4. Earphone B. The homograph is ear. The expression "having an ear" for music means an awareness and talent. (Van Gogh had only one ear.)

GA1304

Homograph Grins

Topic: Action and Reaction

Homograph Grins activities are intended to aid in developing the vocabulary/comprehension skill of interpreting homographs. Words which are **spelled** the same but have different **meanings** are often called **homographs.** Because of these identical spellings but different meanings (and sometimes different pronunciations), often the reader or listener miscommunicates. The following activities help develop an awareness of the multiple meanings of selected words. Work them and have fun!

A. HOMOGRAPH RIDDLES. Read and answer the following riddles. What is the homograph in each one?
1. Why did the prisoner take a shower before breaking out of jail?
2. What happened when the nail and the tire had a fight?
3. What is the best thing to take when you are run down?
4. How are bachelors and detergents alike?
5. What will happen if you don't pay your exorcist?

B. HOMOGRAPH CROSSWORD PUZZLE. Fill in the puzzle at the right with homographs which fit the clues given below.

1		2		3
4				

Across: 4. Whether a guy ends up with a nest egg or goose egg depends upon what kind of _____ he has.

Down: 1. To find cards on ships, look on the _____.
2. After liars die, they lie _____.
3. For bare facts, you must have the _____ truth.

She's on another line right now. Why don't you caw back later?

C. HOMOGRAPH CARTOONS. Can you determine the two different meanings of the homograph in the cartoon at the left?

Answers: A. 1. To make a clean getaway (Clean) 2. The nail knocked the tire flat. (Flat) 3. The license number of the car that hit you (Run down) 4. They both work fast and leave no rings. (Rings) 5. You will be repossessed. B. Across: 4. Chick Down: 1. Decks 2. Still 3. Naked C. The homograph is line. The two kinds are a telephone line and an electrical (power) line.

GA1304

Homograph Grins

Topic: Animal Antics

Homograph Grins activities are intended to aid in developing the vocabulary/comprehension skill of interpreting homographs. Words which are **spelled** the same but have different **meanings** are often called **homographs.** Because of these identical spellings but different meanings (and sometimes different pronunciations), often the reader or listener miscommunicates. The following activities help develop an awareness of the multiple meanings of selected words. Work them and have fun!

A. HOMOGRAPH RIDDLES. Read and answer the following riddles. What is the homograph in each one?

1. Why did the turtle cross the street?
2. If a dog loses its tail, where can he get another?
3. What is the best year for a kangaroo?
4. What do you call a small goat?
5. What has four legs and flies?

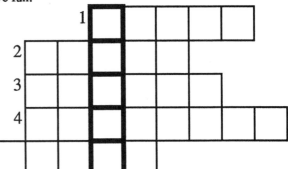

B. HOMOGRAPH PUZZLE. Fill in the puzzle spaces (above) with homographs which should go in the following blanks. (The word framed in the bold squares going down will be the answer to the riddle, "What do you use to raise a baby elephant?")

1. Some farmers use a toothbrush on their cow's teeth so they will give dental _____.
2. A cow wears a bell because its _____ don't work.
3. The young horse had been severely injured, but now is in _____ condition.
4. The cow that goes "Beeeeeeeeep Beeeeeeeeep" is a _____.
5. The kind of dog that is very interested in sports is a _____.

C. HOMOGRAPH CARTOONS. Can you determine the two different meanings of the homograph in the cartoon at the right?

Answers: A. 1. To get to the Shell station (Shell) 2. At the retail shop (Retail) 3. Leap year (Leap) 4. A peanut butter (Peanut, Butter) 5. A dead horse, a picnic table, or two pairs of trousers (Flies)
B. 1. Cream 2. Horns 3. Stable 4. Longhorn 5. Boxer (Crane) C. The homograph is gross. One meaning is twelve dozen or 144 things. Another meaning is indecent, vulgar, or shameful.

GA1304

Homograph Grins

Topic: "The Eyes Have It"

Homograph Grins activities are intended to aid in developing the vocabulary/comprehension skill of interpreting homographs. Words which are **spelled** the same but have different **meanings** are often called **homographs.** Because of these identical spellings but different meanings (and sometimes different pronunciations), often the reader or listener miscommunicates. The following activities help develop an awareness of the multiple meanings of selected words. Work them and have fun!

A. HOMOGRAPH RIDDLES. Read and answer the following riddles. What is the homograph in each one?

1. Why did the athlete blink his eyelashes all day?
2. What is an optometrist's greatest fear?

B. HOMOGRAPH VISIONS.
A "homograph vision" is a drawing of a *misunderstood* homograph. See if you can determine what word or expression was originally said to create each inappropriate "vision" at the right.

Have your eyes been checked lately?

No, they've always been plain brown.

C. HOMOGRAPH CARTOONS. Can you determine the two different meanings of the homograph in the cartoon at the left?

Answers: A. 1. He needed batting practice. (Batting) 2. That he will fall into his lens grinder and make a spectacle of himself (Spectacle) B. 1. Eyeballs 2. Buckeye C. The homograph is checked.

GA1304

Homograph Grins

Topic: Sports Shorts

Homograph Grins activities are intended to aid in developing the vocabulary/comprehension skill of interpreting homographs. Words which are **spelled** the same but have different **meanings** are often called **homographs.** Because of these identical spellings but different meanings (and sometimes different pronunciations), often the reader or listener miscommunicates. The following activities help develop an awareness of the multiple meanings of selected words. Work them and have fun!

A. HOMOGRAPH RIDDLES. Read and answer the following riddles. What is the homograph in each one?
1. What should a prizefighter drink?
2. Why didn't the right fielder get to dance with Cinderella?
3. Why was Cinderella such a poor football player?
4. How do you keep cool at a football game?
5. What is a baseball dog?

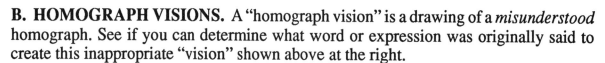

B. HOMOGRAPH VISIONS. A "homograph vision" is a drawing of a *misunderstood* homograph. See if you can determine what word or expression was originally said to create this inappropriate "vision" shown above at the right.

> Why did you bring an extra sock?

> Just in case I get a hole in one.

C. HOMOGRAPH CARTOONS. Can you determine the two different meanings of the homograph in the cartoon at the left?

Homograph Grins

Topic: A Hand-y Arm-y

Homograph Grins activities are intended to aid in developing the vocabulary/comprehension skill of interpreting homographs. Words which are **spelled** the same but have different **meanings** are often called **homographs.** Because of these identical spellings but different meanings (and sometimes different pronunciations), often the reader or listener miscommunicates. The following activities help develop an awareness of the multiple meanings of selected words. Work them and have fun!

A. HOMOGRAPH RIDDLES. Read and answer the following riddles. What is the homograph in each one?
1. Why did the one-handed woman cross the road?
2. How could you describe an octopus going to battle?

B. HOMOGRAPH VISIONS. A "homograph vision" is a drawing of a *misunderstood* homograph. See if you can determine what word or expression was originally said to create each inappropriate "vision" shown below.

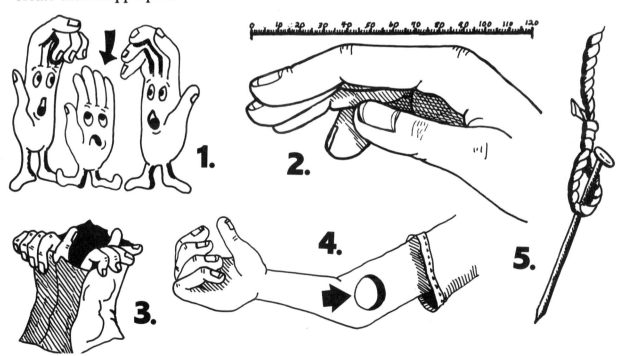

Answers: A. 1. To get to the secondhand shop (Hand) 2. Well-armed (Armed) B. 1. Shorthand 2. Longhand 3. Handbag 4. Armhole 5. Hangnail

GA1304

Homograph Grins

Topic: People and Places

Homograph Grins activities are intended to aid in developing the vocabulary/comprehension skill of interpreting homographs. Words which are **spelled** the same but have different **meanings** are often called **homographs**. Because of these identical spellings but different meanings (and sometimes different pronunciations), often the reader or listener miscommunicates. The following activities help develop an awareness of the multiple meanings of selected words. Work them and have fun!

A. HOMOGRAPH RIDDLES. Read and answer the following riddles. What is the homograph in each one?

1. What kind of make-up do Louisiana majorettes use?
2. What do you have when a boy in Russia gets up in the morning and gets ready for school?
3. When was tennis mentioned in the Bible?
4. What do you call someone who tends sheep in Germany?
5. Why was the United Nations worried when a waiter dropped a plate of turkey on the floor?

B. HOMOGRAPH SEARCH. Fill in the following blanks with words which are homographs. Then find those homographs either down or across in the puzzle at the right.

1. Mickey Mouse went to outer space to find _____.
2. People at a dude ranch generally _____ around.
3. The first day of Adam's life was long because it had no _____.
4. After flying on the magic carpet, Ali Baba felt _____.
5. All statues of George Washington are standing because he would never _____.
6. A girl who has several boyfriends named William is a _____ collector.
7. The hippie went to the North Pole to see other _____ people.
8. Little Bo Peep lost her sheep because she had a _____ with her.
9. George Washington isn't smiling on the dollar bill because he was _____.

```
B E V E C O T
A C R O O K R
P L U T O H U
L B I L L O G
I M J O Y R G
E R U I N S E
O F R A M E D
```

Here lies:
Humpty Dumpty
Cause of death:
Shell Shock

C. HOMOGRAPH CARTOONS. Can you determine the two different meanings of the homograph in the cartoon at the right?

Answers: A. 1. Baton Rouge (Rouge) 2. Russian dressing (Dressing) 3. When Joseph served in Pharaoh's court (Served, Court) 4. A German shepherd (Shepherd) 5. It meant the fall of Turkey, the ruin of Greece and the breakup of China. B. 1. Pluto 2. Horse 3. Eve 4. Rugged 5. Lie 6. Bill 7. Cool 8. Crook 9. Framed C. The homographs are shell and shock.

GA1304

Homograph Grins

Topic: Food for Thought

Homograph Grins activities are intended to aid in developing the vocabulary/comprehension skill of interpreting homographs. Words which are **spelled** the same but have different **meanings** are often called **homographs.** Because of these identical spellings but different meanings (and sometimes different pronunciations), often the reader or listener miscommunicates. The following activities help develop an awareness of the multiple meanings of selected words. Work them and have fun!

A. HOMOGRAPH RIDDLES. Read and answer the following riddles. What is the homograph in each one?
1. What did one potato chip say to the other?
2. What cake makes its own eggs?
3. How can you have bread if you're on a liquid diet?
4. What do geese get when they eat too many sweets?
5. What do you get when two strawberries meet?

```
U S E R V E M
S Q U A R E U
S Q U A S H S
C O R N E A T
U S W E E T A
T H A N K S R
S T A M P E D
```

B. HOMOGRAPH SEARCH. Fill in the following blanks with words which are homographs. Then find those homographs either down or across in the word search puzzle above at the right.
1. The hippie starved to death because he refused to have a _____ meal.
2. _____ always stays hot in the refrigerator.
3. A vegetable always found in crowded buses is the _____.
4. The girl put the sugar under her pillow because she wanted to have _____ dreams.
5. A riot broke out in the post office when a date _____ on a letter.
6. The cannibal was reading a book entitled "How to _____ Your Fellow Man."
7. The lady didn't like _____ flakes because they made so much noise in her shoes.
8. The Band-Aids™ were kept in the refrigerator for cold _____.

C. HOMOGRAPH CARTOONS. Can you determine the two different meanings of the homograph in the cartoon at the right?

Poor Humpty! He's not all he's cracked up to be!

Answers: A. 1. "Let's go for a dip." (Dip) 2. A layer cake (Layer) 3. Drink a toast. (Toast) 4. Goose pimples (Goose) 5. A strawberry shake (Shake) B. 1. Square 2. Mustard 3. Squash 4. Sweet 5. Stamped 6. Serve 7. Corn 8. Cuts C. The homograph is cracked. One meaning is "broken so that the surface is fissured." In the expression "not all it was cracked up to be," the word cracked means praised or glorified.

GA1304

Homograph Grins

Topic: Heads Up!

Homograph Grins activities are intended to aid in developing the vocabulary/comprehension skill of interpreting homographs. Words which are **spelled** the same but have different **meanings** are often called **homographs.** Because of these identical spellings but different meanings (and sometimes different pronunciations), often the reader or listener miscommunicates. The following activities help develop an awareness of the multiple meanings of selected words. Work them and have fun!

A. HOMOGRAPH RIDDLES. Read and answer the following riddles. What is the homograph in each one?

1. What has fifty heads but cannot think?
2. What happens if a cube of sugar falls on your head?
3. What did the wig say to the head?
4. What should you do if you find some liniment that makes your arm smart?

B. HOMOGRAPH VISIONS. A "homograph vision" is a drawing of a *misunderstood* homograph. See if you can determine what word or expression was originally said to create each inappropriate "vision" below.

Answers: A. 1. A box of matches (Heads) 2. You get a lump. (Lump) 3. "I've got you covered." (Covered) 4. Rub some on your head. (Smart) B. 1. Letterhead 2. Cabbage head 3. Headlight

GA1304

Homograph Grins

Topic: Career Concerns

Homograph Grins activities are intended to aid in developing the vocabulary/comprehension skill of interpreting homographs. Words which are **spelled** the same but have different **meanings** are often called **homographs.** Because of these identical spellings but different meanings (and sometimes different pronunciations), often the reader or listener miscommunicates. The following activities help develop an awareness of the multiple meanings of selected words. Work them and have fun!

A. HOMOGRAPH RIDDLES. Read and answer the following riddles. What is the homograph in each one?
1. What should you know if you plan to be a real estate salesman?
2. What could you call a dogcatcher?
3. Why did the elevator operator get depressed?
4. Why can an archaeologist never be successful?
5. How did the electrician feel when all the lights in his building blew out?

B. HOMOGRAPH VISIONS. A "homograph vision" is a drawing of a *misunderstood* homograph. See if you can determine what word or expression was originally said to create this inappropriate "vision" shown at the right.

C. HOMOGRAPH CARTOONS. Can you determine the two different meanings of the homograph in the cartoon at the left?

Homograph Grins

Topic: You Can __BANK__ on It!

Homograph Grins activities are intended to aid in developing the vocabulary/comprehension skill of interpreting homographs. Words which are **spelled** the same but have different **meanings** are often called **homographs.** Because of these identical spellings but different meanings (and sometimes different pronunciations), often the reader or listener miscommunicates. The following activities help develop an awareness of the multiple meanings of selected words. Work them and have fun!

A. HOMOGRAPH PUZZLE. Fill in the puzzle spaces going across (at the right) with homographs which could go in the following blanks:

1. Eskimos keep their money in a _____.
2. The bank clerk climbed a tree because he wanted to become a _____ manager.
3. The tightrope walker always carried his bank book in order to check his _____.
4. The best pattern for a banker's suit is _____.
5. The lady stood next to the vault in the bank because she wanted to be on the _____ side.

The word formed in the bold squares going **down** will be the answer to the following riddle: A river is rich because it has two _____.

B. HOMOGRAPH VISIONS. A "homograph vision" is a drawing of a *misunderstood* homograph. See if you can determine what word or expression was originally said to create this inappropriate "vision" shown at the left.

Answers: A. 1. Snowbank 2. Branch 3. Balance 4. Checks 5. Safe B. Holding up a bank (The homograph is holding.)

GA1304

Homograph Grins

Topic: "Clothes-Out"

Homograph Grins activities are intended to aid in developing the vocabulary/comprehension skill of interpreting homographs. Words which are **spelled** the same but have different **meanings** are often called **homographs.** Because of these identical spellings but different meanings (and sometimes different pronunciations), often the reader or listener miscommunicates. The following activities help develop an awareness of the multiple meanings of selected words. Work them and have fun!

A. HOMOGRAPH RIDDLES. Read and answer the following riddles. What is the homograph in each one?

1. What did one shoelace say to the other?
2. What did the necktie say to the hat?
3. What kind of ties can't you wear?
4. Why did the man's pants look very sad?
5. How did the race between the two shirt collars end?
6. What runs around town all day and lies under the bed at night with its tongue hanging out?

```
B A N D   C U P
L O U D   O R A
U J O Y A U N
E F O O T N S
H A N G U P S
A L A S T H E
C L O S E N D
```

B. HOMOGRAPH SEARCH. Fill in the following blanks with words which are homographs. Then find those homographs either down or across in the puzzle above at the right.

1. To keep from falling asleep, Silly Sally wore _____ socks.
2. The saddest piece of clothing is the _____ jeans.
3. Uncle Silly wore his hat over his ears so he could hear the ____.
4. A shoe is always one _____ long.
5. One stocking said to the other, "So long now, I gotta _____."
6. A dog wears a _____ all winter and _____ in the summer.
7. Empty closets have no _____.

C. HOMOGRAPH CARTOONS. Can you determine the two different meanings of the homograph in the cartoons at the right?

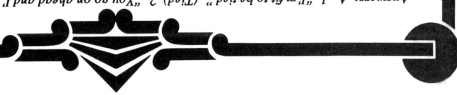

Homograph Grins

Topic: Keeping Your Head Together

Homograph Grins activities are intended to aid in developing the vocabulary/comprehension skill of interpreting homographs. Words which are **spelled** the same but have different **meanings** are often called **homographs**. Because of these identical spellings but different meanings (and sometimes different pronunciations), often the reader or listener miscommunicates. The following activities help develop an awareness of the multiple meanings of selected words. Work them and have fun!

A. HOMOGRAPH RIDDLES. Read and answer the following riddles. What is the homograph in each one?
1. What pierces ears without leaving a hole?
2. Why was the lady's hair angry?
3. What can you do about a constant ringing in your ears?
4. What did one tonsil say to the other?

B. HOMOGRAPH VISIONS. A "homograph vision" is a drawing of a *misunderstood* homograph. See if you can determine what word or expression was originally said to create each inappropriate "vision."

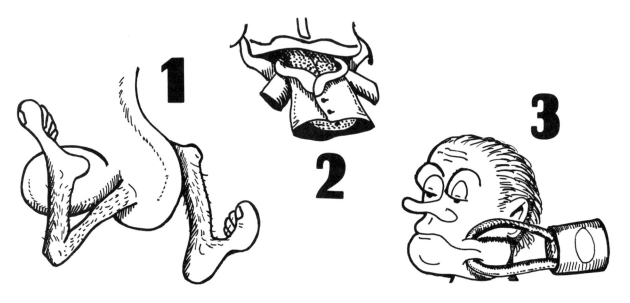

Answers: A. 1. Noise (Pierces) 2. It was always being teased. (Teased) 3. Get an unlisted telephone number. (Ringing) 4. "Get dressed! The doctor's taking us out!" (Out) B. 1. A running nose 2. A coated tongue 3. Lockjaw

GA1304

TRIPLE TROUBLE CARD 1
OPPOSITES: Give the opposite of each of the following words.

Night

Boy

Back

TRIPLE TROUBLE CARD 2
PLURALS: Give the spelling of the plural form of each of the following singular words.

Child

Ox

Girl

TRIPLE TROUBLE CARD 3
INITIALS: Rather than saying a full word or phrase, initials are frequently used. What initials might be used for each of the following?

Television

Postscript

District attorney

TRIPLE TROUBLE CARD 4
SINGULAR: Give the spelling of the singular form of each of the following plural words.

Women

Streets

Dice

TRIPLE TROUBLE CARD 5
BACKWARD WORDS: What would each of the following words be when spelled backwards?

Stop

Ward

Won

TRIPLE TROUBLE CARD 6
ABBREVIATIONS: Give the spelling (and punctuation) for the abbreviations of each of the following words.

Sunday

Quart

Street

TRIPLE TROUBLE CARD 7
CONTRACTIONS: What words should be written if the apostrophes were removed from each of the following contractions?

They're

Here's

O'clock

TRIPLE TROUBLE CARD 8
ABBREVIATIONS: The following are three abbreviations. Give the full word for each one.

Nov.

Jr.

Mr.

TRIPLE TROUBLE CARD 9
NUMBER OF SYLLABLES: Give the number of syllables in each of the following words.

Ago

Strengths

Area

TRIPLE TROUBLE CARD 10
WORDS RHYMING WITH <u>AT</u>: The following describes words which rhyme with **at.** What is each word?

A feline

An insect

A rodent

TRIPLE TROUBLE CARD 11
WORDS ENDING WITH -RN: The following describes words which end with **-rn.** What is each word?

A vegetable

Thick thread

To grieve

TRIPLE TROUBLE CARD 12
WORDS WITH LONG <u>O</u> SOUND: The following describes words which contain the long o sound. What is each word?

An outer garment

Not fast

Not closed

TRIPLE TROUBLE CARD 13
WORDS BEGINNING WITH <u>STR</u>-: The following describes words which begin with **str-.** What is each word?

A road

Powerful

A fruit

TRIPLE TROUBLE CARD 14
WORDS WITH SHORT <u>E</u> SOUND: The following describes words which contain the short e sound. What is each word?

Damp

Santa's helper

A number

TRIPLE TROUBLE CARD 15
ANALOGIES: Complete the following analogies. (Read **:** "is to" and **::** "as." Example: *In is to out as hot is to* _____.)

In : out :: hot : ___

She : her :: he : ___

Ice : cold :: sun : ___

TRIPLE TROUBLE Card 3 Answers:	TRIPLE TROUBLE Card 2 Answers:	TRIPLE TROUBLE Card 1 Answers:
TV PS DA	Children Oxen Girls	Day Girl Front
TRIPLE TROUBLE Card 6 Answers:	TRIPLE TROUBLE Card 5 Answers:	TRIPLE TROUBLE Card 4 Answers:
Sun. Qt. St.	Pots Draw Now	Woman Street Die
TRIPLE TROUBLE Card 9 Answers:	TRIPLE TROUBLE Card 8 Answers:	TRIPLE TROUBLE Card 7 Answers:
2 1 3	November Junior Mister	They are Here is Of the clock
TRIPLE TROUBLE Card 12 Answers:	TRIPLE TROUBLE Card 11 Answers:	TRIPLE TROUBLE Card 10 Answers:
Coat Slow Open	Corn Yarn Mourn	Cat Gnat Rat
TRIPLE TROUBLE Card 15 Answers:	TRIPLE TROUBLE Card 14 Answers:	TRIPLE TROUBLE Card 13 Answers:
Cold Him/his Hot	Wet Elf 7,10,11, or 12	Street Strong Strawberry

GA1304

TRIPLE TROUBLE CARD 16

WORDS BEGINNING WITH SN-: Each of the following phrases defines a word which begins with **sn-**. What are the words?

A reptile

A rough breathing noise during sleep

The nose of a beast

TRIPLE TROUBLE CARD 17

NUMBER WORDS: The following definitions of words have to do with numbers. What are the words?

Four singers

Group of twelve

Three-sided figure

TRIPLE TROUBLE CARD 18

EXPRESSIONS—THE WEATHER: Words pertaining to weather occur in various expressions. Fill in the blanks with words pertaining to weather.

Right as _____

Soft as a _____

It never _____ but it pours.

TRIPLE TROUBLE CARD 19

PERIOD: By adding a period to some words, they become abbreviations. If a period were added to each of these words, what would the abbreviation stand for?

Gal

In

Jan

TRIPLE TROUBLE CARD 20

COMPOUND WORDS: A compound word is a combination of two different words. The following phrases define compound words beginning with **black.** What are they?

Name of a fruit

A reptile

A period of darkness

TRIPLE TROUBLE CARD 21

EXPRESSIONS—ANIMALS: There are many names of animals in various expressions which we use frequently. Fill in the following blanks with the names of animals.

Eager _____

_____ pecked

Road _____

TRIPLE TROUBLE CARD 22

ADD A LETTER: In each row of three words, the same letter can be added at the beginning to create three new words. What is each letter?

_eat, _troll, _weep

_lane, _recede, _our

_hick, _ill, _read

TRIPLE TROUBLE CARD 23

COLORS: What colors do we associate with the following things?

Being cowardly

A revolutionary

In good health

TRIPLE TROUBLE CARD 24

HOMOPHONES: Homophones are words which sound alike but have different spellings and meanings. **Spell** a homophone for each of the following words.

I

In

Be

TRIPLE TROUBLE CARD 25

APOSTROPHES: If an apostrophe appeared in a particular place in the following words, they would be different words altogether. What would they be?

Id

Cant

Wont

TRIPLE TROUBLE CARD 26

HOMOPHONES: Homophones are words which sound alike but have different spellings and meanings. **Spell** a homophone for each of the following words.

Our

Made

New

TRIPLE TROUBLE CARD 27

PARTS OF SPEECH: The following are three parts of speech with the vowel letters omitted. What are they?

ntrjctn

djctv

prpstn

TRIPLE TROUBLE CARD 28

ANIMAL NOISES: Cows "moo," but what "noises" do we generally say are made by the animals below?

Turkeys

Frogs

Doves

TRIPLE TROUBLE CARD 29

FAMOUS PAIRS: Many words occur in pairs. Complete each of the following pairs.

Dick and _____

Bacon and _____

Peaches and _____

TRIPLE TROUBLE CARD 30

SIMILES: A simile is a comparison of two things using **like** or **as.** Complete the following similes with the names of birds or animals.

Blind as a _____

As the _____ flies

Eyes like a _____

TRIPLE TROUBLE
Card 18
Answers:

Rain
Cloud
Rains

TRIPLE TROUBLE
Card 17
Answers:

Quartet
Dozen
Triangle

TRIPLE TROUBLE
Card 16
Answers:

Snake
Snore
Snout

TRIPLE TROUBLE
Card 21
Answers:

Beaver
Hen
Hog

TRIPLE TROUBLE
Card 20
Answers:

Blackberry
Blacksnake
Blackout

TRIPLE TROUBLE
Card 19
Answers:

Gallon
Inch
January

TRIPLE TROUBLE
Card 24
Answers:

Eye/aye
Inn
Bee

TRIPLE TROUBLE
Card 23
Answers:

Yellow
Red
Pink

TRIPLE TROUBLE
Card 22
Answers:

S
P
T

TRIPLE TROUBLE
Card 27
Answers:

Interjection
Adjective
Preposition

TRIPLE TROUBLE
Card 26
Answers:

Hour
Maid
Knew

TRIPLE TROUBLE
Card 25
Answers:

I'd
Can't
Won't

TRIPLE TROUBLE
Card 30
Answers:

Bat
Crow
Hawk

TRIPLE TROUBLE
Card 29
Answers:

Jane
Eggs
Cream

TRIPLE TROUBLE
Card 28
Answers:

Gobble
Croak
Coo

GA1304

TRIPLE TROUBLE CARD 31
NUMBER WORDS: The following definitions of words have to do with numbers. What are the words?

Two people singing together

Five children born together

Seven days

TRIPLE TROUBLE CARD 32
EXPRESSIONS—ANIMALS: Fill in the following blanks with the names of animals.

That's a _____ of a different color.

A _____ in hand is worth two in the bush.

Don't count your _____ before they hatch.

TRIPLE TROUBLE CARD 33
SIMILES: A simile is a comparison of two things using **like** or **as.** Complete the following similes with the names of animals.

Stubborn as a _____

Sly as a _____

Poor as a church _____

TRIPLE TROUBLE CARD 34
ANTONYMS: Antonyms are words that have opposite meanings. The following words all have antonyms that rhyme with **rain.** What are they?

Loss

Insane

Fancy

TRIPLE TROUBLE CARD 35
HOMOPHONES: Homophones are words which sound alike but have different spellings and meanings. **Spell** a homophone for each of the following words.

Ate

Road

Hear

TRIPLE TROUBLE CARD 36
COMPOUND WORDS: A compound word is a combination of two different words. The following phrases define compound words beginning with **red.** What are they?

A bird

A British Revolutionary War soldier

A tree

TRIPLE TROUBLE CARD 37
FAMOUS PAIRS: Many words occur in pairs. Complete each of the following pairs.

Mutt and _____

Cain and _____

Jack and _____

TRIPLE TROUBLE CARD 38
AN EXTRA LETTER: Add one extra letter to the word on the left to come up with a new word fitting the definition following that word.

Cut—pretty

Din—to eat

Sun—submerged

TRIPLE TROUBLE CARD 39
EXPRESSIONS—ANIMALS: There are many names of animals in various expressions which we use frequently. Fill in the following blanks with the names of animals.

_____ sense

_____ Latin

_____ love

TRIPLE TROUBLE CARD 40
COMPOUND WORDS: A compound word is a combination of two different words. The following phrases define compound words beginning with **sun.** What are they?

A day of the week

Light from the sun

Descent of sun below horizon

TRIPLE TROUBLE CARD 41
NUMBER WORDS: The following definitions of words have to do with numbers. What are the words?

A two-week period

Two thousand pounds

Ten years

TRIPLE TROUBLE CARD 42
SIMILES: A simile is a comparison of two things using **like** or **as.** Complete the following similes with the names of birds or animals.

Quiet as a _____

Meek as a _____

Bald as an _____

TRIPLE TROUBLE CARD 43
GROUPS: A group of sheep is called a flock. What is a group of each of the following called?

Cows

Fish

Bees

TRIPLE TROUBLE CARD 44
HOMOPHONES: Homophones are words which sound alike but have different spellings and meanings. **Spell** a homophone for each of the following words.

Bear

See

Week

TRIPLE TROUBLE CARD 45
UP: The word **up** is in many expressions which we use often. The following are definitions of expressions which include the word **up.** What are they?

To rob a store

To become happier

Picture of a pretty girl

GA1304

TRIPLE TROUBLE
Card 33
Answers:

Mule
Fox
Mouse

TRIPLE TROUBLE
Card 32
Answers:

Horse
Bird
Chickens

TRIPLE TROUBLE
Card 31
Answers:

Duet
Quintuplets
Week

TRIPLE TROUBLE
Card 36
Answers:

Redbreast/wing/bird
Redcoat
Redwood/bud

TRIPLE TROUBLE
Card 35
Answers:

Eight
Rode
Here

TRIPLE TROUBLE
Card 34
Answers:

Gain
Sane
Plain

TRIPLE TROUBLE
Card 39
Answers:

Horse
Pig
Puppy

TRIPLE TROUBLE
Card 38
Answers:

Cute
Dine
Sunk

TRIPLE TROUBLE
Card 37
Answers:

Jeff
Abel
Jill

TRIPLE TROUBLE
Card 42
Answers:

Mouse
Lamb
Eagle

TRIPLE TROUBLE
Card 41
Answers:

Fortnight
Ton
Decade

TRIPLE TROUBLE
Card 40
Answers:

Sunday
Sunlight/shine
Sunset/down

TRIPLE TROUBLE
Card 45
Answers:

Hold up
Cheer up
Pinup

TRIPLE TROUBLE
Card 44
Answers:

Bare
Sea
Weak

Triple Trouble
Answers
Card 43

Herd
School
Swarm/hive

GA1304

TRIPLE TROUBLE CARD 46
ABBREVIATIONS: What do the following abbreviations stand for?

a.m.

r.f.d.

tbsp.

TRIPLE TROUBLE CARD 47
EXPRESSIONS—ANIMALS: There are many names of animals in various expressions. Fill in the following blanks with the names of animals.

Let sleeping _____ lie.

It's raining _____ and _____.

The _____ can't change its spots.

TRIPLE TROUBLE CARD 48
EXPRESSIONS—FOODS: There are many names of food in various expressions. Fill in the blanks with the name of something to eat or drink.

Don't cry over spilt _____

One bad _____ will ruin the barrel

Don't put all your _____ in one basket

TRIPLE TROUBLE CARD 49
APOSTROPHES: If an apostrophe appeared in a particular place in the following words, they would be different words altogether. What would they be?

Shell

Shed

Were

TRIPLE TROUBLE CARD 50
HOMOPHONES: Homophones are words which sound alike but have different spellings and meanings. **Spell** a homophone for each of the following words.

Nun

Hoes

Doe

TRIPLE TROUBLE CARD 51
FAMOUS PAIRS: Many words occur in pairs. Complete each of the following pairs.

Romeo and _____

Punch and _____

Sugar and _____

TRIPLE TROUBLE CARD 52
COMPOUND WORDS: A compound word is a combination of two different words. The following phrases define compound words beginning with **house.** What are they?

Something to wear

Roof

A married woman in charge of a household

TRIPLE TROUBLE CARD 53
SIMILES: A simile is a comparison of two things using **like** or **as.** Complete the following similes with the names of birds or animals.

Scarce as _____'s teeth

As funny as a barrel of _____

Slick as a greased _____

TRIPLE TROUBLE CARD 54
HOMOPHONES: Homophones are words which sound alike but have different spellings and meanings. **Spell** a homophone for each of the following words.

Slay

Rose

Past

TRIPLE TROUBLE CARD 55
EXPRESSIONS—ANIMALS: There are many names of animals in various expressions which we use frequently. Fill in the following blanks with the names of animals.

_____ in the grass

To smell a _____

Buy a _____ in a poke

TRIPLE TROUBLE CARD 56
AN EXTRA LETTER: Add one extra letter to the word on the left to come up with a new word fitting the definition following that word.

Cold—to fuss

Team—water vapor

Own—a dress

TRIPLE TROUBLE CARD 57
ANTONYMS: Antonyms are words that have opposite meanings. The following words all have antonyms that rhyme with **so.** What are they?

Fast

Yes

Stop

TRIPLE TROUBLE CARD 58
FAMOUS PAIRS: Many words occur in pairs. Complete each of the following pairs.

Amos and _____

Fine and _____

Black and _____

TRIPLE TROUBLE CARD 59
BOOK TITLES: The following are titles of children's books with the vowel letters omitted. What are they?

Bmb

Hd

Sndr

TRIPLE TROUBLE CARD 60
SIMILES: A simile is a comparison of two things using **like** or **as.** Complete the following similes with the names of food.

Thick as _____ _____

Slow as _____

Bald as a peeled _____

TRIPLE TROUBLE
Card 48
Answers:

Milk
Apple
Eggs

TRIPLE TROUBLE
Card 47
Answers:

Dogs
Cats/dogs
Leopard

TRIPLE TROUBLE
Card 46
Answers:

Before noon (ante meridian)
Rural Free Delivery
Tablespoon

TRIPLE TROUBLE
Card 51
Answers:

Juliet
Judy
Spice

TRIPLE TROUBLE
Card 50
Answers:

None
Hose
Dough

TRIPLE TROUBLE
Card 49
Answers:

She'll
She'd
We're

TRIPLE TROUBLE
Card 54
Answers:

Sleigh
Rows
Passed

TRIPLE TROUBLE
Card 53
Answers:

Hen's
Monkeys
Pig

TRIPLE TROUBLE
Card 52
Answers:

Housecoat
Housetop
Housewife

TRIPLE TROUBLE
Card 57
Answers:

Slow
No
Go

TRIPLE TROUBLE
Card 56
Answers:

Scold
Steam
Gown

TRIPLE TROUBLE
Card 55
Answers:

Snake
Rat
Pig

TRIPLE TROUBLE
Card 60
Answers:

Pea soup
Molasses
Onion

TRIPLE TROUBLE
Card 59
Answers:

Bambi
Heidi
Sounder

TRIPLE TROUBLE
Card 58
Answers:

Andy
Dandy
White

GA1304

TRIPLE TROUBLE CARD 61

-GRAPH-: The root word **-graph-** means to write. The following are definitions of words with **-graph-**. What are they?

A picture

An instrument for playing records

Life's story written by the person himself

TRIPLE TROUBLE CARD 62

ADD A LETTER: In each set of three words the same letter can be added at the beginning to create three new and different words. What is each letter?

_are, __ear, __our

__luster, __eel, __ox

__ace, __each, __ark

TRIPLE TROUBLE CARD 63

SIMILES: A simile is a comparison of two things using **like** or **as**. Complete the following similes with colors.

_____ as snow

_____ as indigo

_____ as a gourd

TRIPLE TROUBLE CARD 64

WORD BLENDS: A word blend is formed by combining parts of two different words. Identify the two original words for each of the following word blends.

Brunch

Smog

Motel

TRIPLE TROUBLE CARD 65

NUMBER WORDS: The prefix **tri-** means three. The following are definitions of words which begin with **tri-**. What are they?

A vehicle with three wheels

Three-fold

A stand with three legs

TRIPLE TROUBLE CARD 66

EXPRESSIONS—ANIMALS: Fill in the following blanks with the names of animals.

The early bird gets the _____.

Take the _____ by the horns.

It's the straw that broke the _____'s back.

TRIPLE TROUBLE CARD 67

PALINDROMES: A palindrome is a word that is spelled the same backwards and forwards. The following are some definitions of three word palindromes. What are they?

Sound of a horn or whistle

The middle of the day

Female sheep

TRIPLE TROUBLE CARD 68

FAMOUS PAIRS: Many words occur in pairs. Complete each of the following pairs.

Horse and _____

Stars and _____

Law and _____

TRIPLE TROUBLE CARD 69

ABBREVIATIONS: What do the following abbreviations stand for?

p.m.

tsp.

in.

TRIPLE TROUBLE CARD 70

NUMBER WORDS: The following definitions of words have to do with numbers. What are the words?

Eight notes on a scale

Four pecks

A hundred years

TRIPLE TROUBLE CARD 71

HOMOPHONES: Homophones are words which sound alike but have different spellings and meanings. **Spell** a homophone for each of the following words.

Heard

Tents

Find

TRIPLE TROUBLE CARD 72

COMPOUND WORDS: A compound word is a combination of two different words. The following phrases define compound words beginning with **book**. What are they?

One who reads a lot

Something to make books stand up

Something to hold one's place in a book

TRIPLE TROUBLE CARD 73

ANTONYMS: Antonyms are words that have opposite meanings. The following words all have antonyms that rhyme with **at**. What are they?

Dog

Skinny

Pointed

TRIPLE TROUBLE CARD 74

EXPRESSIONS—PARTS OF THE BODY: Names of parts of the body occur frequently in various expressions. Fill in the blanks with names of parts of the body.

Keep your _____ peeled.

The cat's got his _____.

Keep your _____ to the grindstone.

TRIPLE TROUBLE CARD 75

HOMOPHONES: Homophones are words which sound alike but have different spellings and meanings. **Spell** a homophone for each of the following words.

Piece

Rain

Him

GA1304

TRIPLE TROUBLE
Card 63
Answers:

White
Blue
Green

TRIPLE TROUBLE
Card 62
Answers:

H or P
F
P or L

TRIPLE TROUBLE
Card 61
Answers:

Photograph
Phonograph
Autobiography

TRIPLE TROUBLE
Card 66
Answers:

Worm
Bull
Camel's

TRIPLE TROUBLE
Card 65
Answers:

Tricycle
Triple/triplicate
Tripod

TRIPLE TROUBLE
Card 64
Answers:

Breakfast & lunch
Smoke & fog
Motor(ist) & hotel

TRIPLE TROUBLE
Card 69
Answers:

Afternoon
(post meridian)
Teaspoon
Inch

TRIPLE TROUBLE
Card 68
Answers:

Buggy
Stripes
Order

TRIPLE TROUBLE
Card 67
Answers:

Toot
Noon
Ewe

TRIPLE TROUBLE
Card 72
Answers:

Bookworm
Bookend/shelf
Bookmark(er)

TRIPLE TROUBLE
Card 71
Answers:

Herd
Tense/tints
Fined

TRIPLE TROUBLE
Card 70
Answers:

Octave
Bushel
Century

TRIPLE TROUBLE
Card 75
Answers:

Peace
Rein/reign
Hem/hymn

TRIPLE TROUBLE
Card 74
Answers:

Eyes
Tongue
Nose

TRIPLE TROUBLE
Card 73
Answers:

Cat
Fat
Flat

TRIPLE TROUBLE CARD 76
CROW: The word **crow** is used as a part of many expressions. What one word or phrase containing **crow** fits the following definitions?

A bar of iron with a crook or claw

In a straight line

Wrinkles at the outer corners of the eye

TRIPLE TROUBLE CARD 77
FAMOUS PAIRS: Many words occur in pairs. Complete each of the following pairs.

Hansel and _____

Curds and _____

Tooth and _____

TRIPLE TROUBLE CARD 78
HOMOPHONES: Homophones are words which sound alike but have different spellings and meanings. **Spell** a homophone for each of the following words.

Seen

Red

Pail

TRIPLE TROUBLE CARD 79
SHORTENED WORDS: Many American words have undergone a shortening process. From what longer words did we get these shorter words?

Doc

Gym

Prof

TRIPLE TROUBLE CARD 80
SIMILES: A simile is a comparison of two things using **like** or **as**. Complete the following similes with the names of animals.

Crooked as a _____'s hind leg

Snug as a _____ in a rug

You're as lazy as a _____ .

TRIPLE TROUBLE CARD 81
NUMBER WORDS: The prefix **bi-** means two. The following are definitions of words which begin with **bi-**. What are they?

A vehicle with two wheels

Glasses with two-part lens

Occurring every two months

TRIPLE TROUBLE CARD 82
ANIMAL NOISES: Cows "moo," but what "noises" do we generally say are made by the animals below?

Hyenas

Crows

Horses

TRIPLE TROUBLE CARD 83
ANTONYMS: Antonyms are words that have opposite meanings. The following words all have antonyms that rhyme with **tin.** What are they?

Lose

Out

Fat

TRIPLE TROUBLE CARD 84
EXPRESSIONS—PARTS OF THE BODY: Names of parts of the body occur frequently in various expressions. Fill in the blanks with names of parts of the body.

Don't lose your _____ .

Put your money where your _____ is.

Sticks and stones will break my _____ but words will never hurt me.

TRIPLE TROUBLE CARD 85
NUMBER WORDS: The prefix **uni-** means one. The following are definitions of words which begin with **uni-**. What are they?

One part

A mythical animal with one horn

An outfit people (such as nurses) wear

TRIPLE TROUBLE CARD 86
SIMILES: A simile is a comparison of two things using **like** or **as**. Complete the following similes with the names of food.

Thick as _____

Cold as _____

Alike as two _____ in a pod

TRIPLE TROUBLE CARD 87
COMPOUND WORDS: A compound word is a combination of two different words. The following phrases define compound words beginning with **black.** What are they?

Extortion by threats

Something to write on

Twenty-one card game

TRIPLE TROUBLE CARD 88
ABBREVIATIONS: What do the following abbreviations stand for?

P.T.A.

T.W.A.

T.L.C.

TRIPLE TROUBLE CARD 89
EXPRESSIONS—PARTS OF THE BODY: Names of parts of the body occur frequently in various expressions. Fill in the blanks with names of parts of the body.

The way to a man's _____ is through his _____ .

You put your _____ in your _____ .

Put your _____ to the plow.

TRIPLE TROUBLE CARD 90
HOMOPHONES: Homophones are words which sound alike but have different spellings and meanings. **Spell** a homophone for each of the following words.

Holy

Least

Fourth

TRIPLE TROUBLE
Card 78
Answers:

Scene
Read
Pale

TRIPLE TROUBLE
Card 77
Answers:

Gretel
Whey
Nail

TRIPLE TROUBLE
Card 76
Answers:

Crowbar
As the crow flies
Crow's feet

TRIPLE TROUBLE
Card 81
Answers:

Bicycle
Bifocals
Bimonthly

TRIPLE TROUBLE
Card 80
Answers:

Dog's
Bug
Hound dog

TRIPLE TROUBLE
Card 79
Answers:

Doctor
Gymnasium
Professor

TRIPLE TROUBLE
Card 84
Answers:

Head
Mouth
Bones

TRIPLE TROUBLE
Card 83
Answers:

Win
In
Thin

TRIPLE TROUBLE
Card 82
Answers:

Laugh
Caw
Neigh/whinny

TRIPLE TROUBLE
Card 87
Answers:

Blackmail
Blackboard
Blackjack

TRIPLE TROUBLE
Card 86
Answers:

Molasses
Kraut
Peas

TRIPLE TROUBLE
Card 85
Answers:

Unit
Unicorn
Uniform

TRIPLE TROUBLE
Card 90
Answers:

Wholly
Leased
Forth

TRIPLE TROUBLE
Card 89
Answers:

Heart/stomach
Foot/mouth
Shoulder

TRIPLE TROUBLE
Card 88
Answers:

Parent-Teacher As-sociation
Trans World Airlines
Tender loving care

TRIPLE TROUBLE CARD 91
JACK WORDS: **Jack** is part of many words or expressions which we use frequently. Tell how **jack** is associated with each of the following descriptions.

Associated with diving

Used at Halloween

Something we'd like to hit someday

TRIPLE TROUBLE CARD 92
BABIES: Many young animals have special names. What is the young animal called for each of the following?

Seal

Whale

Tiger

TRIPLE TROUBLE CARD 93
MALE AND FEMALE: What is the female counterpart for the following male terms?

Lion

Bull

Gander

TRIPLE TROUBLE CARD 94
DOUBLE TALK: Some English words and expressions are made up of two parts that are exactly alike, such as the word **bonbon.** What are the double parts of those defined below?

Father

A prison in New York

A type of loose fitting dress

TRIPLE TROUBLE CARD 95
ABBREVIATIONS: What do the following abbreviations stand for?

T.G.I.F.

U.S.N.

Ph.D.

TRIPLE TROUBLE CARD 96
HOMOPHONES: Homophones are words which sound alike but have different spellings and meanings. **Spell** a homophone for each of the following words.

Claws

Coarse

Mist

TRIPLE TROUBLE CARD 97
WORD BLENDS: A word blend is formed by combining parts of two different words. Identify the two original words for each of the following word blends.

Splatter

Bookmobile

Prissy

TRIPLE TROUBLE CARD 98
COMPOUND WORDS: A compound word is a combination of two different words. The following phrases define compound words beginning with **sun.** What are they?

A browning of the skin

An instrument to show the time of day

Inflammation of the skin caused by overexposure to sunlight

TRIPLE TROUBLE CARD 99
UP: The word **up** is used in many expressions which we use daily. The following are definitions of expressions which include the word **up.** What are they?

Confused

To reverse direction

To reach someone ahead of you

TRIPLE TROUBLE CARD 100
HOMOPHONES: Homophones are words which sound alike but have different spellings and meanings. **Spell** a homophone for each of the following words.

Grown

Hole

Wood

TRIPLE TROUBLE CARD 101
FAMOUS PAIRS: Many words occur in pairs. Complete each of the following pairs.

Chapter and _____

Antony and _____

Mason and _____

TRIPLE TROUBLE CARD 102
COLORS: What colors do we associate with the following things?

Envy

Purity

Melancholy songs

TRIPLE TROUBLE CARD 103
EXPRESSIONS—ANIMALS: There are many names of animals in various expressions which we use frequently. Fill in the following blanks with the names of animals.

See you later _____.

I'll be a _____'s uncle.

You can lead a _____ to water, but you can't make him drink.

TRIPLE TROUBLE CARD 104
APOSTROPHES: If an apostrophe appeared in a particular place in the following words, they would be different words altogether. What would they be?

Wed

Ill

Well

TRIPLE TROUBLE CARD 105
EXPRESSIONS—ANIMALS: There are many names of animals in various expressions which we use frequently. Fill in the following blanks with the names of animals.

Lord love a _____

It's a _____'s life.

Drunk as a _____

TRIPLE TROUBLE
Card 93
Answers:

Lioness
Cow
Goose

TRIPLE TROUBLE
Card 92
Answers:

Pup
Calf
Cub

TRIPLE TROUBLE
Card 91
Answers:

Jackknife
Jack-o'-lantern
Jackpot

TRIPLE TROUBLE
Card 96
Answers:

Clause
Course
Missed

TRIPLE TROUBLE
Card 95
Answers:

Thank God it's Friday
United States Navy
Doctor of Philosophy

TRIPLE TROUBLE
Card 94
Answers:

Papa
Sing Sing
Muumuu

TRIPLE TROUBLE
Card 99
Answers:

Mixed up
Back up
Catch up

TRIPLE TROUBLE
Card 98
Answers:

Suntan
Sundial
Sunburn

TRIPLE TROUBLE
Card 97
Answers:

Splash and spatter
Book and automobile
Prim and sissy

TRIPLE TROUBLE
Card 102
Answers:

Green
White
Blue

TRIPLE TROUBLE
Card 101
Answers:

Verse
Cleopatra
Dixon

TRIPLE TROUBLE
Card 100
Answers:

Groan
Whole
Would

TRIPLE TROUBLE
Card 105
Answers:

Duck
Dog's
Skunk

TRIPLE TROUBLE
Card 104
Answers:

We'd
I'll
We'll

TRIPLE TROUBLE
Card 103
Answers:

Alligator
Monkey's
Horse

GA1304

TRIPLE TROUBLE CARD 106
PALINDROMES: A palindrome is a word that is spelled the same backwards and forwards. The following are definitions of palindromes. What are they?

Energy

A title for a lady

Protective cloth worn under the chin

TRIPLE TROUBLE CARD 107
WORDS WITH THE SAME PARTS: In each set of compound expressions below, half of the expression is missing. The same word fits each blank in the row. What is the word for each row?

___stop, ___cut, ___cake

___boat, ___fly, ___maid

Horse___, fire___, dragon___

TRIPLE TROUBLE CARD 108
NUMBER WORDS: The prefix bi- means two. The following are definitions of words which begin with bi-. What are they?

Having two sides

An animal with two feet

Person having two husbands or wives

TRIPLE TROUBLE CARD 109
-GRAPH-: The root word -graph- means to write. The following are definitions of words containing -graph-. What are they?

The written story of someone's life

A study of earth, land, and sea

A written signature by the person himself

TRIPLE TROUBLE CARD 110
NUMBER WORDS: The prefix bi- means two. The following are definitions of words which begin with bi-. What are they?

To cut into two equal parts

Speaking two languages

Occurring every two weeks

TRIPLE TROUBLE CARD 111
EXPRESSIONS—ANIMALS: There are many names of animals in various expressions which we use frequently. Fill in the following blanks with the names of animals.

_____ court

To earn a _____ skin

To eat _____

TRIPLE TROUBLE CARD 112
FOREIGN NUMBERS: The following are numbers under ten in a foreign language. What are the numbers?

Dos (Spanish)

Sechs (German)

Quatre (French)

TRIPLE TROUBLE CARD 113
HOMOPHONES: Homophones are words which sound alike but have different spellings and meanings. **Spell** a homophone for each of the following words.

Threw

Throne

Pain

TRIPLE TROUBLE CARD 114
EXPRESSIONS—PARTS OF THE BODY: Names of parts of the body occur frequently in various expressions. Fill in the blanks with names of parts of the body.

Two _____ are better than one.

I have it on the tip of my _____.

Don't bite the _____ that feeds you.

TRIPLE TROUBLE CARD 115
GROUPS: A group of sheep is called a flock. What is a group of each of the following called?

Wolves

Kittens

Lions

TRIPLE TROUBLE CARD 116
NUMBER WORDS: The prefix mono- means one. The following are definitions of words which begin with mono-. What are they?

One syllable

An oxide containing one atom of oxygen

Speech by one person

TRIPLE TROUBLE CARD 117
EXPRESSIONS—FOODS: There are many names of foods in various expressions which we use frequently. Fill in each blank with the name of something to eat.

It wouldn't cut hot _____.

It's like taking _____ from a baby.

It's as easy as _____.

TRIPLE TROUBLE CARD 118
AN EXTRA LETTER: Add one extra letter somewhere to the word on the left to form a new word fitting the definition following that word.

Ten—shelter made of canvas

Wad—a division of a hospital

Her—a man admired for his bravery

TRIPLE TROUBLE CARD 119
HOMOPHONES: Homophones are words which sound alike but have different spellings and meanings. **Spell** a homophone for each of the following words.

Vein

Wait

One

TRIPLE TROUBLE CARD 120
SHORTENED WORDS: Many American words have undergone a shortening process. From what longer words did we get these shorter words?

Ad

Exam

Still

GA1304

TRIPLE TROUBLE
Card 108
Answers:

Bilateral
Biped
Bigamist

TRIPLE TROUBLE
Card 107
Answers:

Short
House
Fly

TRIPLE TROUBLE
Card 106
Answers:

Pep
Madam
Bib

TRIPLE TROUBLE
Card 111
Answers:

Kangaroo
Sheep
Crow

TRIPLE TROUBLE
Card 110
Answers:

Bisect
Bilingual
Biweekly

TRIPLE TROUBLE
Card 109
Answers:

Biography
Geography
Autograph

TRIPLE TROUBLE
Card 114
Answers:

Heads
Tongue
Hand

TRIPLE TROUBLE
Card 113
Answers:

Through
Thrown
Pane

TRIPLE TROUBLE
Card 112
Answers:

Two
Six
Four

TRIPLE TROUBLE
Card 117
Answers:

Butter
Candy
Pie

TRIPLE TROUBLE
Card 116
Answers:

Monosyllable
Monoxide
Monolog

TRIPLE TROUBLE
Card 115
Answers:

Pack
Litter/kindle
Pride

TRIPLE TROUBLE
Card 120
Answers:

Advertisement
Examination
Distill

TRIPLE TROUBLE
Card 119
Answers:

Vain/vane
Weight
Won

TRIPLE TROUBLE
Card 118
Answers:

Tent
Ward
Hero

GA1304

TRIPLE TROUBLE CARD 121	TRIPLE TROUBLE CARD 122	TRIPLE TROUBLE CARD 123
ACRONYMS: Acronyms are words formed by combining the initial letters or syllables of several words. What are the words from which the following acronyms were made? **Nabisco** **Nasa** **Radar**	**FOREIGN NUMBERS:** The following are numbers under ten in a foreign language. What are they? **Uno (Spanish)** **Sept (French)** **Tres (Spanish)**	**HOMOPHONES:** Homophones are words which sound alike but have different spellings and meanings. **Spell** a homophone for each of the following words. **Flour** **Presents** **Ring**
TRIPLE TROUBLE CARD 124	TRIPLE TROUBLE CARD 125	TRIPLE TROUBLE CARD 126
WORD BLENDS: A word blend is formed by combining parts of two different words. Identify the two original words for each of the following word blends. **Electrocute** **Chortle** **Travelogue**	**NUMBER WORDS:** The prefix **uni-** means one. The following are definitions of words which begin with **uni-**. What are they? **A vehicle with one wheel** **One-sided** **To join together as one**	**ANAGRAMS:** Anagrams are words made by rearranging the letters of other words. Rearrange the letters in the words on the left to form a new word which fits the definition provided. **Live—wicked or bad** **Stop—a blot or stain** **Tame—a food**
TRIPLE TROUBLE CARD 127	TRIPLE TROUBLE CARD 128	TRIPLE TROUBLE CARD 129
MALAPROPISMS: A malapropism is an incorrect wording which sounds almost right. What is incorrect with the following, and how **should** each be said? **Mary was Joseph's exposed wife.** **Please guard against cosmetic rays.** **Our principal is a very extinguished man.**	**NUMBER WORDS:** The prefix **mono-** means one. The following are definitions of words which begin with **mono-**. What are they? **An eyeglass for one eye** **One tone** **Exclusive control of one commodity**	**HOMOGRAPHS:** Homographs are words spelled alike but different in meaning and sometimes pronunciation. These are two different definitions of a homograph. What are they? **To conduct—a metal** **A movement of air—to twist** **To rip—a drop of water from the eye**
TRIPLE TROUBLE CARD 130	TRIPLE TROUBLE CARD 131	TRIPLE TROUBLE CARD 132
-DUC(E)-: Many words can be formed by adding prefixes to the root word **-duc(e)-**. The following are definitions of three such words. What are they? **To make smaller or lessen** **Person in charge of a train** **One who finances a motion picture**	**HOMOPHONES:** Homophones are words which sound alike but have different spellings and meanings. **Spell** a homophone for each of the following words. **Patience** **Principle** **Morning**	**ETYMOLOGY:** Words in our language have come from several other languages. From which language was each of the following sets of words derived? **Soprano, Madonna** **Camouflage, Ballet** **Adobe, Cigar**
TRIPLE TROUBLE CARD 133	TRIPLE TROUBLE CARD 134	TRIPLE TROUBLE CARD 135
PHOBIAS: The meaning of the word **phobia** is fear of. What are people with the following phobias afraid of? **Claustrophobia** **Autophobia** **Toxicophobia**	**COMPOUND WORDS:** A compound word is a combination of two different words. The following phrases define compound words beginning with **house**. What are they? **A barge used as a dwelling** **A party to celebrate taking possession of a house** **An insect**	**GOOD-BY:** The following are three words for **good-by.** From what language did each come? **Adios** **Au revoir** **Arrive derci**

GA1304

TRIPLE TROUBLE
Card 123
Answers:

Flower
Presence
Wring

TRIPLE TROUBLE
Card 122
Answers:

One
Seven
Three

TRIPLE TROUBLE
Card 121
Answers:

National Biscuit Company
National Aeronautics and Space Administration
Radio detecting and ranging

TRIPLE TROUBLE
Card 126
Answers:

Evil/vile
Spot
Meat

TRIPLE TROUBLE
Card 125
Answers:

Unicycle
Unilateral
Unite

TRIPLE TROUBLE
Card 124
Answers:

Electricity and execute
Chuckle and snort
Travel and monologue

TRIPLE TROUBLE
Card 129
Answers:

Lead
Wind
Tear

Triple Trouble
Card 128
Answers:

Monocle
Monotone
Monopoly

TRIPLE TROUBLE
Card 127
Answers:

Exposed/espoused
Cosmetic/cosmic
Extinguished/distinguished

TRIPLE TROUBLE
Card 132
Answers:

Italian
French
Spanish

TRIPLE TROUBLE
Card 131
Answers:

Patients
Principal
Mourning

TRIPLE TROUBLE
Card 130
Answers:

Reduce
Conductor
Producer

TRIPLE TROUBLE
Card 135
Answers:

Spanish
French
Italian

TRIPLE TROUBLE
Card 134
Answers:

Houseboat
Housewarming
Housefly

TRIPLE TROUBLE
Card 133
Answers:

Closed places
Being alone
Poisons

GA1304

WORD TWISTER
Card 1
The meaning of what word was twisted to cause someone to imagine the picture below?

WORD TWISTER
Card 2
The meaning of what word was twisted to cause someone to imagine the picture below?

WORD TWISTER
Card 3
The meaning of what word was twisted to cause someone to imagine the picture below?

WORD TWISTER
Card 4
The meaning of what word was twisted to cause someone to imagine the picture below?

WORD TWISTER
Card 5
The meaning of what word was twisted to cause someone to imagine the picture below?

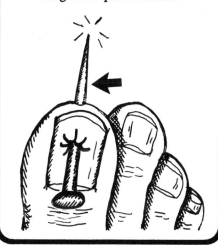

WORD TWISTER
Card 6
The meaning of what word was twisted to cause someone to imagine the picture below?

WORD TWISTER
Card 7
The meaning of what word was twisted to cause someone to imagine the picture below?

WORD TWISTER
Card 8
The meanings of what two words were twisted to cause someone to imagine the picture below?

WORD TWISTER
Card 9
The meaning of what word was twisted to cause someone to imagine the picture below?

GA1304

WORD TWISTER
Card 10
The meaning of what word was twisted to cause someone to imagine the picture below?

WORD TWISTER
Card 11
The meaning of what word was twisted to cause someone to imagine the picture below?

WORD TWISTER
Card 12
The meaning of what word was twisted to cause someone to imagine the picture below?

WORD TWISTER
Card 13
The meaning of what word was twisted to cause someone to imagine the picture below?

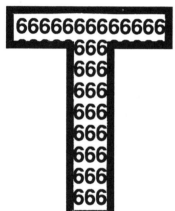

WORD TWISTER
Card 14
The meaning of what word was twisted to cause someone to imagine the picture below?

WORD TWISTER
Card 15
The meaning of what word was twisted to cause someone to imagine the picture below?

WORD TWISTER
Card 16
The meaning of what word was twisted to cause someone to imagine the picture below?

WORD TWISTER
Card 17
The meaning of what word was twisted to cause someone to imagine the picture below?

WORD TWISTER
Card 18
The meaning of what word was twisted to cause someone to imagine the picture below?

GA1304

WORD TWISTER
Card 19
The meaning of what word was twisted to cause someone to imagine the picture below?

WORD TWISTER
Card 20
The meaning of what word was twisted to cause someone to imagine the picture below?

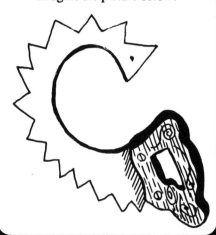

WORD TWISTER
Card 21
The meaning of what word was twisted to cause someone to imagine the picture below?

WORD TWISTER
Card 22
The meaning of what word was twisted to cause someone to imagine the picture below?

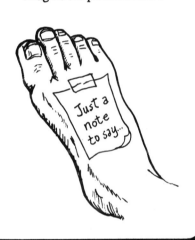

WORD TWISTER
Card 23
The meaning of what word was twisted to cause someone to imagine the picture below?

WORD TWISTER
Card 24
The meaning of what word was twisted to cause someone to imagine the picture below?

WORD TWISTER
Card 25
The meaning of what word was twisted to cause someone to imagine the picture below?

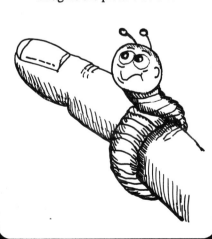

WORD TWISTER
Card 26
The meaning of what word was twisted to cause someone to imagine the picture below?

WORD TWISTER
Card 27
The meaning of what word was twisted to cause someone to imagine the picture below?

GA1304

WORD TWISTER
Card 28
The meaning of what word was twisted to cause someone to imagine the picture below?

WORD TWISTER
Card 29
The meaning of what word was twisted to cause someone to imagine the picture below?

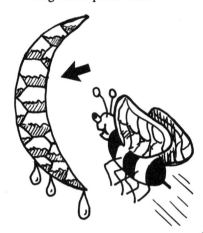

WORD TWISTER
Card 30
The meaning of what word was twisted to cause someone to imagine the picture below?

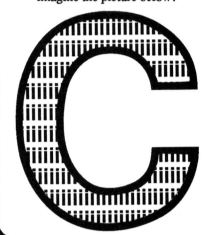

WORD TWISTER
Card 31
The meaning of what word was twisted to cause someone to imagine the picture below?

WORD TWISTER
Card 32
The meaning of what word was twisted to cause someone to imagine the picture below?

WORD TWISTER
Card 33
The meaning of what word was twisted to cause someone to imagine the picture below?

WORD TWISTER
Card 34
The meaning of what word was twisted to cause someone to imagine the picture below?

WORD TWISTER
Card 35
The meaning of what word was twisted to cause someone to imagine the picture below?

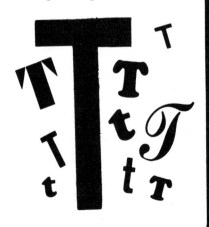

WORD TWISTER
Card 36
The meaning of what word was twisted to cause someone to imagine the picture below?

GA1304

WORD TWISTER
Card 37
The meaning of what word was twisted to cause someone to imagine the picture below?

WORD TWISTER
Card 38
The meaning of what word was twisted to cause someone to imagine the picture below?

WORD TWISTER
Card 39
The meaning of what word was twisted to cause someone to imagine the picture below?

WORD TWISTER
Card 40
The meaning of what word was twisted to cause someone to imagine the picture below?

WORD TWISTER
Card 41
The meaning of what word was twisted to cause someone to imagine the picture below?

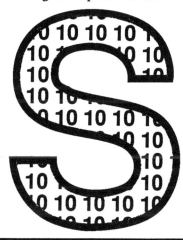

WORD TWISTER
Card 42
The meaning of what word was twisted to cause someone to imagine the picture below?

WORD TWISTER
Card 43
The meaning of what word was twisted to cause someone to imagine the picture below?

WORD TWISTER
Card 44
The meaning of what word was twisted to cause someone to imagine the picture below?

WORD TWISTER
Card 45
The meanings of what two words were twisted to cause someone to imagine the picture below?

GA1304

WORD TWISTER
Card 46

The meaning of what word was twisted to cause someone to imagine the picture below?

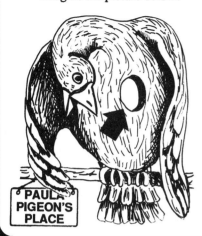

PAULA PIGEON'S PLACE

WORD TWISTER
Card 47

The meaning of what word was twisted to cause someone to imagine the picture below?

WORD TWISTER
Card 48

The meaning of what word was twisted to cause someone to imagine the picture below?

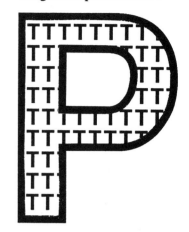

WORD TWISTER
Card 49

The meanings of what two words were twisted to cause someone to imagine the picture below?

A PAGE ABOUT RAMS

WORD TWISTER
Card 50

The meaning of what word was twisted to cause someone to imagine the picture below?

WORD TWISTER
Card 51

The meaning of what word was twisted to cause someone to imagine the picture below?

WORD TWISTER
Card 52

The meaning of what word was twisted to cause someone to imagine the picture below?

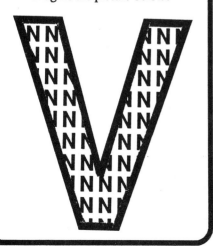

WORD TWISTER
Card 53

The meaning of what word was twisted to cause someone to imagine the picture below?

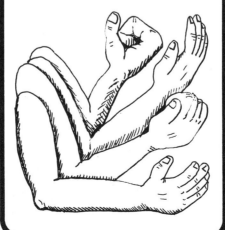

WORD TWISTER
Card 54

The meaning of what word was twisted to cause someone to imagine the picture below?

N N N
N
N
N
N
N N N

GA1304

WORD TWISTER
Card 55

The meanings of what two words were twisted to cause someone to imagine the picture below?

WORD TWISTER
Card 56

The meaning of what word was twisted to cause someone to imagine the picture below?

VERB
VERB
VERB
+VERB

WORD TWISTER
Card 57

The meaning of what word was twisted to cause someone to imagine the picture below?

WORD TWISTER
Card 58

The meaning of what word was twisted to cause someone to imagine the picture below?

WORD TWISTER
Card 59

The meaning of what word was twisted to cause someone to imagine the picture below?

WORD TWISTER
Card 60

The meaning of what word was twisted to cause someone to imagine the picture below?

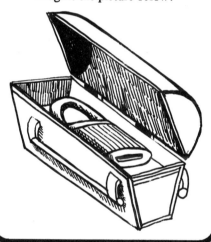

WORD TWISTER
Card 61

The meaning of what word was twisted to cause someone to imagine the picture below?

WORD TWISTER
Card 62

The meaning of what word was twisted to cause someone to imagine the picture below?

WORD TWISTER
Card 63

The meaning of what word was twisted to cause someone to imagine the picture below?

GA1304

WORD TWISTER
Card 64
The meaning of what word was twisted to cause someone to imagine the picture below?

WORD TWISTER
Card 65
The meaning of what word was twisted to cause someone to imagine the picture below?

WORD TWISTER
Card 66
The meaning of what word was twisted to cause someone to imagine the picture below?

WORD TWISTER
Card 67
The meaning of what word was twisted to cause someone to imagine the picture below?

WORD TWISTER
Card 68
The meaning of what word was twisted to cause someone to imagine the picture below?

WORD TWISTER
Card 69
The meaning of what word was twisted to cause someone to imagine the picture below?

WORD TWISTER
Card 70
The meaning of what word was twisted to cause someone to imagine the picture below?

WORD TWISTER
Card 71
The meaning of what word was twisted to cause someone to imagine the picture below?

WORD TWISTER
Card 72
The meaning of what word was twisted to cause someone to imagine the picture below?

GA1304

WORD TWISTER
Card 73
The meaning of what word was twisted to cause someone to imagine the picture below?

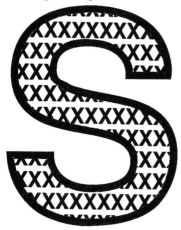

WORD TWISTER
Card 74
The meaning of what word was twisted to cause someone to imagine the picture below?

WORD TWISTER
Card 75
The meaning of what word was twisted to cause someone to imagine the picture below?

WORD TWISTER
Card 76
The meaning of what word was twisted to cause someone to imagine the picture below?

WORD TWISTER
Card 77
The meaning of what word was twisted to cause someone to imagine the picture below?

WORD TWISTER
Card 78
The meaning of what word was twisted to cause someone to imagine the picture below?

WORD TWISTER
Card 79
The meaning of what word was twisted to cause someone to imagine the picture below?

WORD TWISTER
Card 80
The meaning of what word was twisted to cause someone to imagine the picture below?

WORD TWISTER
Card 81
The meaning of what word was twisted to cause someone to imagine the picture below?

GA1304

Vocabulary Vivacity Words Rhyming with MAY	Vocabulary Vivacity Words Rhyming with END	Vocabulary Vivacity Words Rhyming with EAT	Vocabulary Vivacity Words Rhyming with CAP
clay	bend	meat	gap
today	spend	sweet	lap
sway	blend	pleat	map
neigh	trend	sheet	scrap
ashtray	attend	preheat	slap
ballet	depend	athlete	kidnap
birthday	boyfriend	complete	kneecap
bouquet	pretend	defeat	mousetrap

Vocabulary Vivacity Words Rhyming with BE	Vocabulary Vivacity Words Rhyming with BELL	Vocabulary Vivacity Words Rhyming with BED	Vocabulary Vivacity Words Rhyming with RAIN
sea	cell	dead	pain
key	shell	bled	brain
flea	smell	said	chain
ski	swell	thread	reign
agree	expel	instead	train
honeybee	hotel	copperhead	airplane
chimpanzee	doorbell	gingerbread	explain
referee	misspell	arrowhead	insane

Vocabulary Vivacity Words Rhyming with EYE	Vocabulary Vivacity Words Rhyming with EAR	Vocabulary Vivacity Words Rhyming with ATE	Vocabulary Vivacity Words Rhyming with AND
pie	clear	gate	band
buy	cheer	plate	sand
try	fear	slate	land
shy	spear	straight	brand
July	reindeer	weight	demand
lullaby	pioneer	locate	expand
multiply	overhear	punctuate	planned
deny	atmosphere	decorate	understand

Vocabulary Vivacity Words Rhyming with GO	Vocabulary Vivacity Words Rhyming with BEAD	Vocabulary Vivacity Words Rhyming with BAR	Vocabulary Vivacity Words Rhyming with MAIL
sew	deed	car	snail
know	lead	far	pale
throw	need	jar	female
rainbow	read	scar	whale
scarecrow	greed	cigar	inhale
tiptoe	stampede	guitar	fingernail
buffalo	agreed	superstar	detail
radio	centipede	handlebar	tattletale

70

GA1304

Vocabulary Vivacity Words Rhyming with BUM	Vocabulary Vivacity Words Rhyming with ROUND	Vocabulary Vivacity Words Rhyming with HOP	Vocabulary Vivacity Words Rhyming with ON
some hum dumb income crumb eardrum thumb chum	found hound pound sound crowned bound playground compound	mop shop swap drop desktop hilltop teardrop mountaintop	con swan coupon baton nylon pecan python Amazon
Vocabulary Vivacity **Words Rhyming with MUG**	**Vocabulary Vivacity** **Words Rhyming with HOT**	**Vocabulary Vivacity** **Words Rhyming with MOON**	**Vocabulary Vivacity** **Words Rhyming with HOLE**
bug dug jug rug hug drug earplug ladybug	pot blot knot swat forgot watt jackpot apricot	prune swoon cartoon baboon cocoon raccoon afternoon tablespoon	goal mole roll control tadpole fishbowl charcoal flagpole
Vocabulary Vivacity **Words Rhyming with FOOD**	**Vocabulary Vivacity** **Words Rhyming with FORT**	**Vocabulary Vivacity** **Words Rhyming with TOOK**	**Vocabulary Vivacity** **Words Rhyming with OAK**
mood feud rude stewed include seafood attitude multitude	sport wart court short airport resort quart deport	cook hook look shook brook fishhook checkbook pocketbook	joke soak broke choke croak smoke slowpoke artichoke
Vocabulary Vivacity **Words Rhyming with TOY**	**Vocabulary Vivacity** **Words Rhyming with BORN**	**Vocabulary Vivacity** **Words Rhyming with BONE**	**Vocabulary Vivacity** **Words Rhyming with ODD**
enjoy joy annoy cowboy destroy corduroy Illinois employ	corn horn torn worn thorn mourn unworn unicorn	loan groan shone throne alone telephone cyclone xylophone	rod nod cod squad plod prod tripod tightwad

Vocabulary Vivacity **Words Rhyming with BLOCK**	**Vocabulary Vivacity** **Words Rhyming with BEAN**	**Vocabulary Vivacity** **Words Rhyming with PILE**	**Vocabulary Vivacity** **Words Rhyming with EASE**
clock	green	mile	tease
knock	clean	file	please
shock	screen	smile	breeze
hemlock	between	I'll	cheese
livestock	machine	style	freeze
roadblock	sardine	reptile	sneeze
shamrock	gasoline	sundial	squeeze
ticktock	seventeen	crocodile	overseas

Vocabulary Vivacity **Words Rhyming with OAT**	**Vocabulary Vivacity** **Words Rhyming with FINE**	**Vocabulary Vivacity** **Words Rhyming with PIECE**	**Vocabulary Vivacity** **Words Rhyming with BOO**
goat	dine	grease	new
wrote	nine	niece	blue
throat	sign	lease	chew
quote	twine	decrease	few
vote	deadline	police	flu
sailboat	grapevine	obese	glue
raincoat	porcupine	release	shoe
footnote	valentine	increase	shampoo

Vocabulary Vivacity **Words Rhyming with EYES**	**Vocabulary Vivacity** **Words Rhyming with IN**	**Vocabulary Vivacity** **Words Rhyming with I'D**	**Vocabulary Vivacity** **Words Rhyming with WET**
wise	win	ride	net
size	thin	hide	debt
prize	grin	bride	sweat
sunrise	skin	slide	threat
surprise	chin	divide	forget
disguise	pin	decide	sunset
advertise	kin	outside	quartet
apologize	violin	satisfied	alphabet

Vocabulary Vivacity **Words Rhyming with LIP**	**Vocabulary Vivacity** **Words Rhyming with ILL**	**Vocabulary Vivacity** **Words Rhyming with ICE**	**Vocabulary Vivacity** **Words Rhyming with BEST**
rip	pill	rice	west
dip	bill	nice	nest
clip	chill	mice	pest
drip	grill	price	vest
filmstrip	shrill	slice	guest
fingertip	until	twice	request
steamship	anthill	advice	suggest
sportsmanship	daffodil	sacrifice	addressed

GA1304

Vocabulary Vivacity
Words Beginning with "Ch-"

chew
chili
charge
chipmunk
chapter
champion
cheap
chapter

Vocabulary Vivacity
Words Beginning with "Cr-"

crawl
crazy
crackers
cradle
cranky
crater
cricket
cremate

Vocabulary Vivacity
Words Beginning with "Gl-"

glad
glass
glue
glossy
glance
glamour
glimpse
gloomy

Vocabulary Vivacity
Words Beginning with "Pl-"

plus
plate
plow
plural
plastic
plan
plaid
pleasant

Vocabulary Vivacity
Words Beginning with "Bl-"

blind
bloom
bluff
blush
blueberry
blade
blister
blizzard

Vocabulary Vivacity
Words Beginning with "Dr-"

dragon
drench
driveway
drought
drowsy
drown
drudgery
dromedary

Vocabulary Vivacity
Words Beginning with "Gr-"

grade
grass
gravy
grapes
grammar
greedy
grouchy
grudge

Vocabulary Vivacity
Words Beginning with "Pr-"

pretty
pride
practice
price
pressure
prefix
prairie
predict

Vocabulary Vivacity
Words Beginning with "Br-"

breeze
bridge
broad
branch
bracelet
breakfast
brilliant
broccoli

Vocabulary Vivacity
Words Beginning with "Fl-"

flame
flake
flock
fleece
flutter
flashlight
flamingo
flattery

Vocabulary Vivacity
Words Beginning with "Kn-"

knee
knife
kneel
knit
knight
knead
knothole
knowledge

Vocabulary Vivacity
Words Beginning with "Sc-"

school
science
scorch
scales
scamper
scallops
scorpion
scholar

Vocabulary Vivacity
Words Beginning with "Cl-"

cloud
clam
clutter
clever
climate
clippers
clumsy
clarinet

Vocabulary Vivacity
Words Beginning with "Fr-"

freeze
freedom
freight
frisky
frantic
fruitcake
frequent
frostbite

Vocabulary Vivacity
Words Beginning with "Ph-"

phone
phonics
photograph
phantom
pheasant
phrase
pharmacy
phobia

Vocabulary Vivacity
Words Beginning with "Scr-"

scream
scrap
screen
scrub
scrape
script
screech
scramble

73

GA1304

Vocabulary Vivacity
Words Beginning with "Sh-"
shell
shower
shadow
shaggy
shallow
shingles
shrill
shuffleboard

Vocabulary Vivacity
Words Beginning with "Sn-"
snoop
sneaky
snob
snuggle
snooze
sneakers
snowflake
snorkel

Vocabulary Vivacity
Words Beginning with "Str-"
strike
strict
stray
strangle
stream
stripe
strive
struggle

Vocabulary Vivacity
Words Beginning with "Tr-"
trade
trap
travel
tremble
triplets
treasure
transport
trustworthy

Vocabulary Vivacity
Words Beginning with "Sk-"
skate
ski
skull
skirt
skeleton
skimpy
sketch
skylark

Vocabulary Vivacity
Words Beginning with "Sp-"
spice
spear
spine
spinach
special
sparrow
span
spacious

Vocabulary Vivacity
Words Beginning with "Sw-"
sweat
sway
swarm
swallow
sweater
swine
switch
swipe

Vocabulary Vivacity
Words Beginning with "Tw-"
twin
twist
twelve
twine
twinkle
twang
tweezers
twilight

Vocabulary Vivacity
Words Beginning with "Sl-"
slow
slender
slang
slaughter
sleepwalker
slippery
slight
slingshot

Vocabulary Vivacity
Words Beginning with "Spr-"
spring
spread
spray
sprain
sprinkle
spry
sprig
spruce

Vocabulary Vivacity
Words Beginning with "Th-"
thin
thief
thorn
third
thick
thought
thaw
thimble

Vocabulary Vivacity
Words Beginning with "Wh-"
whisper
wheelbarrow
whistle
wheeze
whiff
whether
whiskers
whippoorwill

Vocabulary Vivacity
Words Beginning with "Sm-"
smile
smooth
smell
smash
smart
smuggle
smother
smolder

Vocabulary Vivacity
Words Beginning with "St-"
storm
stumble
sturdy
stable
stadium
stampede
starvation
stalagmite

Vocabulary Vivacity
Words Beginning with "Thr-"
three
thread
threat
throne
through
thrifty
thrush
thrill

Vocabulary Vivacity
Words Beginning with "Wr-"
wring
wrong
wrist
wren
wreath
wreck
wrench
wrestle

GA1304

Vocabulary Vivacity
Kitchen Words

can
oven
boil
menu
skillet
cabinet
fry
hamburger

Vocabulary Vivacity
Mealtime Words

soup
lunch
dessert
dinner
manners
sandwich
breakfast
leftovers

Vocabulary Vivacity
School Words

principal
library
student
grade
bus
cafeteria
teacher
office

Vocabulary Vivacity
Things We Read

maps
road signs
billboards
labels
menus
mail
recipes
thermometers

Vocabulary Vivacity
Yard Words

rake
tree
mower
shovel
shrub
leaves
ladder
wheelbarrow

Vocabulary Vivacity
Family Words

brother
maid
mailman
children
parents
visitor
neighbor
butler

Vocabulary Vivacity
Prefix "Re-" Words

rerun
retire
repeat
reduce
report
request
repair
resign

Vocabulary Vivacity
Types of Books

catalog
dictionary
encyclopedia
notebook
comic book
telephone book
almanac
atlas

Vocabulary Vivacity
Furniture Words

bed
table
sofa
lamp
shelf
stool
chair
television

Vocabulary Vivacity
Four-Letter Words

girl
hand
sink
book
lion
desk
cars
beef

Vocabulary Vivacity
Parts of a Book

index
contents
chapter
page
words
glossary
preface
pictures

Vocabulary Vivacity
Word Study

synonyms
prefixes
homophones
abbreviations
antonyms
homographs
contractions
syllables

Vocabulary Vivacity
Chore Words

dusting
mopping
sweeping
ironing
cooking
washing
sewing
vacuuming

Vocabulary Vivacity
Music Words

piano
record
bass
sharp
organ
soprano
drums
flat

Vocabulary Vivacity
Printed Materials

books
stories
songs
poems
plays
letters
newspapers
magazines

Vocabulary Vivacity
Public Speaking Terms

speech
accent
pronunciation
posture
gestures
volume
audience
applause

GA1304

Vocabulary Vivacity Library Terms	Vocabulary Vivacity Music/Language Terms	Vocabulary Vivacity Music/Science Terms	Vocabulary Vivacity Word Palindromes
books	accent	valve	tot
card catalog	voice	stem	did
title card	notes	rock	toot
librarian	pitch	organ	noon
dictionary	play	frog	pop
author card	mute	wind	eve
encyclopedia	theme	coil	peep
fines	composition	pulse	level

Vocabulary Vivacity Grammar Terms	Vocabulary Vivacity Music/Action Terms	Vocabulary Vivacity Music/Math Terms	Vocabulary Vivacity Science "A-" Words
noun	stand	triangle	acid
question	slide	quarter	artery
subject	pluck	measure	absorb
adjective	rest	half	amoeba
sentence	snare	meter	abdomen
possessive	horn	whole	atmosphere
verb	fiddle	ledger	atom
pronoun	string	interval	amphibian

Vocabulary Vivacity Things We Write	Vocabulary Vivacity Music/Sports Terms	Vocabulary Vivacity Computer Terms	Vocabulary Vivacity Science "B-" Words
love notes	pitch	printer	blood
business letters	score	keyboard	brain
spelling words	run	command	bacteria
paragraphs	beat	screen	breath
thank-you notes	tie	data	battery
reports	hold	disk	bones
invitations	staff	software	biology
short stories	major	memory	barometer

Vocabulary Vivacity Punctuation Marks	Vocabulary Vivacity Music/Object Terms	Vocabulary Vivacity Emotion Words	Vocabulary Vivacity Science "C-" Words
question mark	pipe	love	cell
period	scales	hate	cocoon
comma	key	joy	cancer
dash	bridge	depression	calcium
colon	reed	fear	chemistry
quotation marks	kettle	anger	calorie
apostrophe	range	sadness	circulation
hyphen	bar	happy	carbohydrates

GA1304

Vocabulary Vivacity
Geography "E-" Words

Earth
east
export
Europe
equator
erosion
empire
elevation

Vocabulary Vivacity
Geography "P-" Words

planet
port
plain
pasture
prairie
pollution
precipitation
Pennsylvania

Vocabulary Vivacity
Math "C-" Words

cent
count
circle
combine
cube
curve
compass
circumference

Vocabulary Vivacity
Math "P-" Words

penny
problem
pound
product
percent
parallel
pentagon
perpendicular

Vocabulary Vivacity
Geography "G-" Words

ground
globe
graph
gulf
gravity
glacier
Georgia
grasslands

Vocabulary Vivacity
Geography "R-" Words

rainfall
range
region
river
route
rural
resources
Rhode Island

Vocabulary Vivacity
Math "D-" Words

dime
digit
distance
divide
dollar
dozen
decimal
diameter

Vocabulary Vivacity
Math "R-" Words

row
round
reduce
rectangle
remainder
ratio
radius
rhombus

Vocabulary Vivacity
Geography "L-" Words

land
lake
level
lava
lagoon
latitude
lowlands
Louisiana

Vocabulary Vivacity
Geography "S-" Words

sea
smog
scale
season
suburb
swamp
survey
South Dakota

Vocabulary Vivacity
Math "F-" Words

fact
feet
figure
fewer
formula
fraction
frequent
Fahrenheit

Vocabulary Vivacity
Math "S-" Words

set
second
shape
side
single
subtract
square
sphere

Vocabulary Vivacity
Geography "M-" Words

map
meadow
mountain
monsoon
meridian
migrant
Maine
Mediterranean

Vocabulary Vivacity
Math "A-" Words

add
amount
angle
area
average
acre
arc
addend

Vocabulary Vivacity
Math "M-" Words

many
measure
middle
mile
minus
multiply
month
metric

Vocabulary Vivacity
Math "T-" Words

time
table
total
ton
triple
triangle
thermometer
teaspoon

Vocabulary Vivacity Science "D-" Words	Vocabulary Vivacity Science "H-" Words	Vocabulary Vivacity Science "O-" Words	Vocabulary Vivacity Science "T-" Words
dew	heat	organ	taste
drugs	heart	oil	test
decay	hatch	orange	trees
desert	horizon	oak	teeth
digest	health	observe	tides
dinosaur	hemisphere	oxygen	thunder
disease	hurricane	ocean	temperature
dolphin	hydrogen	ozone	telescope

Vocabulary Vivacity Science "E-" Words	Vocabulary Vivacity Science "I-" Words	Vocabulary Vivacity Science "P-" Words	Vocabulary Vivacity Science "V-" Words
ear	ice	pulse	vein
egg	insects	pollen	voice
energy	iron	plants	vibrate
eclipse	inhale	protein	valve
extinct	infection	pulley	vapor
evaporate	intestines	purify	virus
experiment	immune	physics	vitamin
electricity	irrigate	pesticide	volcano

Vocabulary Vivacity Science "F-" Words	Vocabulary Vivacity Science "L-" Words	Vocabulary Vivacity Science "R-" Words	Vocabulary Vivacity Science "W-" Words
fish	leaf	rust	water
fog	lens	rocks	weight
fruit	liquid	rice	weather
flower	lungs	roots	well
fins	life	reptile	whale
fossil	light	reflex	wilt
fuel	liver	research	work
fertilizer	laboratory	refrigeration	windpipe

Vocabulary Vivacity Science "G-" Words	Vocabulary Vivacity Science "M-" Words	Vocabulary Vivacity Science "S-" Words	Vocabulary Vivacity Geography "C-" Words
gas	melt	sun	coast
grain	moon	soil	cliff
germ	mold	skin	canyon
gland	mammal	solid	crops
gravity	mercury	senses	canal
glacier	microscope	stomach	crater
gene	moisture	steam	continent
gills	muscle	salamander	California

78

GA1304

Antonym Cartoon 1

Find a pair of antonyms in the cartoon at the right. (Remember that antonyms are words which have opposite meanings.) What are the meanings of the antonyms in this cartoon?

Antonym Cartoon 2

Find a pair of antonyms in the cartoon at the right. (Remember that antonyms are words which have opposite meanings.) What are the meanings of the antonyms in this cartoon?

Antonym Cartoon 3

Find a pair of antonyms in the cartoon at the right. (Remember that antonyms are words which have opposite meanings.) What are the meanings of the antonyms in this cartoon?

GA1304

Answer for Antonym Cartoon 1

The antonyms in this cartoon are **bad** and **good. Bad** means evil, wrong, or not good. **Good** means desirable, favorable, or not bad. The cat in the chair actually had no news at all, neither bad nor good.

Answer for Antonym Cartoon 2

The antonyms in this cartoon are **outside** and **inside. Outside** means outdoors or not inside. **Inside** means within a structure or building, the interior part, or not outside. There will be showers inside this cat household because of the leaks in the ceiling and the outside rains seeping in.

Answer for Antonym Cartoon 3

The antonyms in this cartoon are **wrong** and **right. Wrong** means not correct or not right. **Right** means correct or opposite of left. Note that the word **right** has two different meanings and therefore has the two opposites, **wrong** and **left.** The misunderstanding of the meaning of **right** caused the humor in this cartoon. The cat had put his shoe on his right (not left) foot, but that was the *wrong* foot for the *left* shoe.

GA1304

Antonym Cartoon 4

Find a pair of antonyms in the cartoon at the right. (Remember that antonyms are words which have opposite meanings.) What are the meanings of the antonyms in this cartoon?

Antonym Cartoon 5

Find a pair of antonyms in the cartoon at the right. (Remember that antonyms are words which have opposite meanings.) What are the meanings of the antonyms in this cartoon?

Antonym Cartoon 6

Find a pair of antonyms in the cartoon at the right. (Remember that antonyms are words which have opposite meanings.) What are the meanings of the antonyms in this cartoon?

GA1304

Answer for Antonym Cartoon 4

The antonyms in this cartoon are **much** and **little**. **Much** means great in quantity. **Little** means in a very small quantity. Note that the expression "too much" is a saying which means completely ridiculous or beyond belief.

Answer for Antonym Cartoon 5

The antonyms are **brothers** and **sisters, aunts** and **uncles,** and **nieces** (and **nephews**). Note that the word **insecticide** means a poison used to kill insects.

Answer for Antonym Cartoon 6

The antonyms in this cartoon are **hero** and **chicken.** A **hero** is one whose deeds cause him to be admired. One meaning of **chicken** is a coward. Note that a hero sandwich is a large sandwich usually consisting of a small loaf of bread or roll cut in half lengthwise and containing ingredients such as meat, cheese, lettuce, and tomatoes. It is sometimes called a submarine.

GA1304

Homophone Cartoon 1

Find a homophone in the cartoon at the right. (Remember that homophones are words that sound alike but have different spellings and meanings.) What are the two spellings and meanings of this pair of homophones?

Homophone Cartoon 2

Find a homophone in the cartoon at the right. (Remember that homophones are words that sound alike but have different spellings and meanings.) What are the two spellings and meanings of this pair of homophones?

Homophone Cartoon 3

Find a homophone in the cartoon at the right. (Remember that homophones are words that sound alike but have different spellings and meanings.) What are the two spellings and meanings of this pair of homophones?

83

GA1304

Answer for Homophone Cartoon 1

The homophones in this cartoon are **bore** and **boar.** A **bore** is a very tiresome person. A **boar** is a male hog.

Answer for Homophone Cartoon 2

The homophones in this cartoon are **paw** and **pa.** A **paw** is the foot of an animal. **Pa** is another word for **father.**

Answer for Homophone Cartoon 3

The homophones in this cartoon are **sew** and **so.** **Sew** means to stitch with a needle and thread. The expression **so-so** means moderately well—neither very good nor very bad.

84

GA1304

Homophone Cartoon 4

Find a homophone in the cartoon at the right. (Remember that homophones are words that sound alike but have different spellings and meanings.) What are the two spellings and meanings of this pair of homophones?

Homophone Cartoon 5

Find a homophone in the cartoon at the right. (Remember that homophones are words that sound alike but have different spellings and meanings.) What are the two spellings and meanings of this pair of homophones?

Homophone Cartoon 6

Find a homophone in the cartoon at the right. (Remember that homophones are words that sound alike but have different spellings and meanings.) What are the two spellings and meanings of this pair of homophones?

GA1304

Answer for Homophone Cartoon 4

The homophones in this cartoon are **chilly** and **chili.** **Chilly** means very cool in temperature. **Chili** is a thick sauce of meat and chilies.

Answer for Homophone Cartoon 5

The homophones in this cartoon are **prints** and **prince.** **Prints** are photographs made from a negative. A **prince** is the son of a king or a male member of a royal family. The line of a once popular song is "Someday my prince will come."

Answer for Homophone Cartoon 6

The homophones in this cartoon are **bale** and **bail.** A **bale** is a large bundle of packages or goods such as hay. **Bail** is the money given to release someone from jail.

GA1304

Homograph Cartoon 1

Find a homograph in the cartoon at the right. (Remember that homographs are words which have the same spellings but have different meanings and sometimes different pronunciations.) What are the two meanings of the homograph in this cartoon?

Homograph Cartoon 2

Find a homograph in the cartoon at the right. (Remember that homographs are words which have the same spellings but have different meanings and sometimes different pronunciations.) What are the two meanings of the homograph in this cartoon?

Homograph Cartoon 3

Find a homograph in the cartoon at the right. (Remember that homographs are words which have the same spellings but have different meanings and sometimes different pronunciations.) What are the two meanings of the homograph in this cartoon?

GA1304

Answer for Homograph Cartoon 1

The homograph in this cartoon is **bug.** One meaning of **bug** is an insect or other small creeping or crawling creature. Another meaning is an unexpected defect, fault, flaw, or imperfection. A person can try to get the "bugs" out of something (such as a recipe) without meaning that there will be insects in the prepared food.

Answer for Homograph Cartoon 2

The homograph in this cartoon is **spell.** One meaning of **spell** is a spoken word or series of words which have magic power. Another meaning is to name or write a series of letters in the correct order of a word. One witch thought the other was asking how a word was spelled rather than trying to discuss the magical power that could be cast upon someone.

Answer for Homograph Cartoon 3

The homograph in this cartoon is **swallow.** One meaning of **swallow** is a small long-winged bird. Another meaning is to take in through the mouth into the stomach. Because the bird in the tree was taking so many gulps, the cat joked about calling it a swallow.

GA1304

Homograph Cartoon 4

Find a homograph in the cartoon at the right. (Remember that homographs are words which have the same spellings but have different meanings and sometimes different pronunciations.) What are the two meanings of the homograph in this cartoon?

Homograph Cartoon 5

Find a homograph in the cartoon at the right. (Remember that homographs are words which have the same spellings but have different meanings and sometimes different pronunciations.) What are the two meanings of the homograph in this cartoon?

Homograph Cartoon 6

Find a homograph in the cartoon at the right. (Remember that homographs are words which have the same spellings but have different meanings and sometimes different pronunciations.) What are the two meanings of the homograph in this cartoon?

GA1304

Answer for Homograph Cartoon 4

The homograph in this cartoon is **shower.** One meaning of **shower** is a party given by friends who bring gifts. Another meaning is a type of bath in which water falls on the body for the purpose of cleaning it. The cat in the cartoon did not understand the first meaning of the word **shower** and therefore thought the girl's friend had never had a bath.

Answer for Homograph Cartoon 5

The homograph in this cartoon is **patient.** One meaning of **patient** is waiting calmly without complaining. Another meaning is a person under medical care or treatment. Did you notice the two boxes on the shelf in this cartoon? One is salt. The other is poison. If the poison were used instead of the salt, then the cat would wind up becoming a patient in a hospital.

Answer for Homograph Cartoon 6

The homograph in this cartoon is **hot.** One meaning of **hot** is having a relatively high temperature. Another meaning is being angry or having a temper. The expression "hot under the collar" means that someone is extremely angry. Did you notice the temperature on the thermometer? There is, however, a difference in being too warm and being angry.

Vocabulary Cartoon 1

Study the cartoon at the right. What is the meaning of the word **escalator**? If the cat on the escalator had known what one was, do you think he would have been in such a predicament? Tell why or why not.

Vocabulary Cartoon 2

Study the cartoon at the right. What is the meaning of the word **amnesia**? How much do you think this doctor knows about amnesia? Why is it not appropriate to ask if someone has had amnesia before?

Vocabulary Cartoon 3

Study the cartoon at the right. What is the meaning of the word **simulation**? Is this word a synonym or an antonym for the word **real**? Can a Santa Claus be a simulation? Tell why or why not.

GA1304

Answer for Vocabulary Cartoon 1

An **escalator** is a power-driven set of stairs arranged like an endless belt. These stairs go up or down continuously. If the cat had known what an escalator was, he might not have tried to go down the "up" stairs.

Answer for Vocabulary Cartoon 2

Amnesia is the loss of memory. A doctor who knows this would not ask a patient with amnesia to "remember" whether or not he or she had had amnesia in the past. One who is suffering from a memory loss will not likely be able to recall such information.

Answer for Vocabulary Cartoon 3

A **simulation** is an imitation or a fake. A simulated Santa Claus would only look like the image of the character, but it would be a fake. Every Santa Claus would be a simulation because the character itself is only a fantasy being.

GA1304

Expression Cartoon 1

The cartoon at the right has an expression "lose your cool." What does this expression mean? Why does the misunderstanding of this expression make the situation in the cartoon funny?

Expression Cartoon 2

The cartoon at the right has an expression "it's raining cats and dogs." What does this expression mean? Why does the misunderstanding of this expression make the situation in the cartoon funny?

Expression Cartoon 3

The cartoon at the right has an expression "you can lead a horse to water, but you can't make him drink." What does this expression mean? Why does the misunderstanding of this expression make the situation in the cartoon funny?

93

GA1304

Answer for Expression Cartoon 1

The expression "lose your cool" is used when someone is no longer calm. Those who have lost their cool are quite annoyed and impatient. The saying does not relate to temperature, as in the refrigerator. The first cat in this cartoon was simply trying to joke with the second cat about "losing his cool."

Answer for Expression Cartoon 2

The expression "it's raining cats and dogs" is often used to describe a very heavy downpour. It does not mean that cats and dogs are actually falling like raindrops from the sky. The expression may have begun when someone compared the accompanying thunder and lightning to a cat and dog fighting. Some say that the expression likely began in old England where there were large holes in the road. After these holes had filled with water from heavy rains, several of the area's numerous dogs and cats fell into these holes, looking as if it had "rained cats and dogs." Others say the expression was due to the accumulation of dead animals in overflowing gutters after heavy rains. The humor in the cartoon is based on the fact that these two cats had heard the expression and were attempting to see for themselves whether or not cats and dogs were actually "raining."

Answer for Expression Cartoon 3

The saying "you can lead a horse to water, but you can't make him drink" means that all of the conditions might be just right for an event or an action to occur, but it still may not happen. For example, if you wanted your baby brother to eat some food you have fixed for him, simply having a hot and delicious meal will not guarantee he will eat it. The "horse" in this cartoon is only a puppet. This allows the cat to use the expression in a humorous manner.

Expression Cartoon 4

The cartoon at the right has an expression "stiff upper lip." What does this expression mean? Why does the misunderstanding of this expression make the situation in the cartoon funny?

Expression Cartoon 5

The cartoon at the right has an expression "money talks." What does this expression mean? Why does the misunderstanding of this expression make the situation in the cartoon funny?

Expression Cartoon 6

The cartoon at the right has an expression "feeling under the weather." What does this expression mean? Why does the misunderstanding of this expression make the situation in the cartoon funny?

GA1304

Answer for Expression Cartoon 4

When someone is asked to keep a "stiff upper lip," it has no association with the actual stiffness of the lip. It is a suggestion to maintain one's courage through a crisis or to try to face some tough times bravely. For example, if a girl has been told she will soon have serious surgery, she might be advised to "keep a stiff upper lip." The cartoon shows a literal stiff upper lip on a cat. This is very different from the meaning when these words are used as an expression.

Answer for Expression Cartoon 5

The folk saying "money talks" means that having money is the same as having power. Although it is not a fact, the saying suggests that money can buy anything or cause anything to happen; therefore, it can "talk." The cat in this cartoon had heard the saying. In order to keep his money from "talking" (and possibly telling someone where it is hiding), he decided to bury it deep enough so no one would be able to hear it.

Answer for Expression Cartoon 6

If one feels "under the weather," he or she feels sick. This generally means feeling queasy or nauseous. This saying could have begun with early travelers on ships who became ill because of the constant motions of the water, particularly during bad weather. It could have continued with air travelers who became ill from the motions of the aircraft, again because of the weather. The cat in this cartoon is shown with a literal translation of the saying.

Expression Cartoon 7

The cartoon at the right has an expression "spreading myself too thin." What does this expression mean? Why does the misunderstanding of this expression make the situation in the cartoon funny?

Expression Cartoon 8

The cartoon at the right has an expression "the pen is mightier than the sword." What does this expression mean? Why does the misunderstanding of this expression make the situation in the cartoon funny?

Expression Cartoon 9

The cartoon at the right has an expression "speak softly and carry a big stick." What does this expression mean? Why does the misunderstanding of this expression make the situation in the cartoon funny?

GA1304

Answer for Expression Cartoon 7

When a person is said to "spread himself (or herself) too thin," it means that person is trying to do too many things at the same time. Usually that individual cannot manage to do these jobs very well. For example, if a boy has baseball practice, a piano lesson, choir practice, a soccer game, a student council meeting, and play rehearsal all on Monday afternoons, he might be spreading himself too thin. The second cat in the cartoon thinks the remark is funny because of the word **thin.** The first cat is quite obviously not too thin.

Answer for Expression Cartoon 8

The saying "the pen is mightier than the sword" means that words (often written with a pen) are often more powerful than physical force (as with a sword). An example might be a newspaper story about a bad deed someone did. The harm done to this person's reputation through this article might be more painful than being stabbed with a sword. The cat in this cartoon did not understand the meaning of the saying and is therefore trying to lift a large pen to see how "mighty" it is.

Answer for Expression Cartoon 9

"Speak softly and carry a big stick" is a saying which means that if one has a powerful weapon, shouting is not necessary. Theodore Roosevelt, the 26th President of the United States, used this expression in connection with his foreign policy. The cat in this cartoon actually reversed this saying by shouting and carrying a small stick.

GA1304

Prefix Meaning:
to, toward

Other Spellings for Prefix:
ac- ad- af- ag-
an- at- as- ap-

Examples:
advise, assistance, application
accepting, attractive, affectionate
attainable, acclamation

Prefix Meaning:
to, toward

Other Spellings for Prefix:
ac- ad- af- ag-
an- at- as- ap-

Examples:
against, assist, attain
advisory, access, aspire
unacceptable, appendage

Prefix Meaning:
to, toward

Other Spellings for Prefix:
ac- ad- af- ag-
an- at- as- ap-

Examples:
acclaim, advise, attend
advantage, addiction, inattention
aspire, aversion

Prefix Meaning:
into, not

Other Spellings:
im- il- ir-

Examples:
include, immobile, imported
injection, irreverent, impulsive
inspirational, inadvisable

Prefix Meaning:
into, not

Other Spellings:
im- il- ir-

Examples:
impress, inspect, imply
inclusion, impending, inference
insensitivity, unimpressive

Prefix Meaning:
into, not

Other Spellings:
im- il- ir-

Examples:
important, infection, impel
inspection, inattention, illogical
inaccessible, inquisition

Prefix Meaning:
with, together

Other Spellings:
co- com- col-

Examples:
combined, conforming, cooperation
contact, compelled, collision
congressional, compression

Prefix Meaning:
with, together

Other Spellings:
co- com- col-

Examples:
collection, constructed, company
coexisting, container, compacted
conservative, compulsion

Prefix Meaning:
with, together

Other Spellings:
co- com- col-

Examples:
conduct, compose, compile
concoction, conquest, continent
conspiracy, convocation

GA1304

GA1304

Prefix Meaning:
not

Examples:
untie, unacceptable, uninformed
undo, unquestionable, unhappy
unreasonable, unproductive

Prefix Meaning:
not

Examples:
unkind, unavoidable, unequalled
unmoved, unintentional, unimpressed
unobjectionable, unpredictability

Prefix Meaning:
not

Examples:
unlike, unknown, unintelligent,
unashamed, undesired, unemotional
unadmitted, unimportantly

Prefix Meaning:
again, back

Examples:
return, refuses, reporting
requested, repulsive, repaint
reply, reinfected

Prefix Meaning:
again, back

Examples:
rerun, referred, recess
revision, respects, reconvened
redeposited, reinspecting

Prefix Meaning:
again, back

Examples:
reduce, unreported, retention
reclaiming, revert, irresistible
reinspired, readmission

Prefix Meaning:
out

Other Spellings for Prefix:

Examples:
except, exported, extractions
edict, eliminate, evoked
efforts, exclamation

Prefix Meaning:
out

Other Spellings for Prefix:

Examples:
extended, edict, excessive
effective, emotion, elude
emotion, unexceptional

Prefix Meaning:
under

Other Spellings for Prefix:

Examples:
suffer, supported, subscriptions
successive, suspensions, submitted
submarine, subvocalizations

GA1304

102

GA1304

Prefix Meaning:
down, away

Examples:
depress, demotion, deformed
dependable, deported, devised
deserving, undescribable

Prefix Meaning:
across

Examples:
transport, transposed, transferring
transducer, transformed, transistor
transgressions, transcriptions

Prefix Meaning:
for, in front of

Examples:
promote, provided, project
productions, protractor, provoke
professors, procedures

Prefix Meaning:
before

Examples:
prepare, prewash, predictable
precooked, prefixes, pretending
prescriptions, predisposition

Prefix Meaning:
between, among

Examples:
intermission, intercepted, interruption
interject, intermediate, interpretations
interdepartmental, interdependency

Prefix Meaning:
not, opposite
apart, away

Other Spellings for Prefix:
di- dif-

Examples:
dislike, different, disclaimed
dismissals, diversions, disrespectable
disassociate, distractions

Prefix Meaning:
down, away

Examples:
defer, detention, dejected
undecided, deduction, declarations
description, decapitate

Prefix Meaning:
through

Examples:
perfect, performances, permission
perspiration, persistence, persuade
perforations, perspective

Prefix Meaning:
against, toward
in the way

Other Spellings for Prefix:
ob- oc-
of- op-

Examples:
omit, object, offer
opposite, overt, oppressive
obsession, offensive

GA1304

-ion

Other Spellings for Suffix:
-tion   -ation
-sion

-ive

Other Spellings for Suffix:
-tive   -ative
-itive   -sive

-er

Other Spellings for Suffix:
-ar   -ir
-or   -ur

-ion

Other Spellings for Suffix:
-tion   -ation
-sion

-ence

Other Spellings for Suffix:
-ance   -ancy
-ency

-able

Other Spellings for Suffix:
-ible   -ble

-ion

Other Spellings for Suffix:
-tion   -ation
-sion

-al

Other Spellings for Suffix:
-ual

-ly

Other Spellings for Suffix:
-ily

GA1304

-s

Other Spellings for Suffix:
-es

-s

Other Spellings for Suffix:
-es

-s

Other Spellings for Suffix:
-es

-ed

Other Spellings for Suffix:
-d

-ed

Other Spellings for Suffix:
-d

-ed

Other Spellings for Suffix:
-d

-ing

-ing

-ing

GA1304

-dict-

Root Meaning:
say, tell

Other Spellings for Root:
-dic-

Examples:
dictionary, predicting, diction
indicted, edict, predicates
unpredictable, indications

-clude-

Root Meaning:
close

Other Spellings for Root:
-clud- -clus-
-cluse-

Examples:
including, precludes, recluse
excluded, conclusions, occluding
seclusive, reclusion

-quest-

Root Meaning:
search, seek, ask

Other Spellings for Root:
-quer- -quis-
-quire- -quir-

Examples:
question, inquired, requesting
inquest, inquisitive, exquisite
requisition, unquestionable

-pel-

Root Meaning:
drive, push

Other Spellings for Root:
-puls- -pell-
-pulse-

Examples:
pulse, propelling, expelled,
dispel, impulsive, compelling
repulsive, propellers

-spect-

Root Meaning:
look

Other Spellings for Root:
-spec- -(x)pect-
-spic-

Examples:
expect, specs, prospect
inspected, spectators, suspecting
unspectacular, conspicuous

-claim-

Root Meaning:
call, cry out

Other Spellings for Root:
-clam-

Examples:
claim, exclaimed, proclaiming
reclaimed, proclamation, unclaimed
exclamatory, disclaimer

-vene-

Root Meaning:
come

Other Spellings for Root:
-ven- -vent-

Examples:
vent, invent, prevent
intervention, reconvene, inventory
conventioneers, preventiveness

-voke-

Root Meaning:
call

Other Spellings for Root:
-vok- -voc-
-voca-

Examples:
vocal, vocabulary, provoke
revoking, invocation, vocation
subvocalization, convocation

-fect-

Root Meaning:
do, make

Other Spellings for Root:
-fec- -fice- -fic-
-fact- -fac-

Examples:
fact, factory, office
infectious, defective, effective
manufacturing, officiate

GA1304

110

-vise-

Root Meaning:
see

Other Spellings for Root:
-vis- -vid-
-vide- -video-

Examples:
videotape, advise, provide
visor, vision, advise
invisible, television

-script-

Root Meaning:
write

Other Spellings for Root:
-scrip- -scrib-
-scribe-

Examples:
scribe, script, inscribe
scribbles, transcribe, description
scriptures, prescriptions

-mote-

Root Meaning:
move

Other Spellings for Root:
-mot- -mob-
-mov- -mobil-
-move- -mobile-

Examples:
move, mobile, promote
demoted, remote, mobilization
immobility, commotion

-posit-

Root Meaning:
put, place

Other Spellings for Root:
-posi- -pos-
-posite- -pose-

Examples:
pose, position, oppose
suppose, impose, composition
opposites, imposition

-ply-

Root Meaning:
fold, use
entwine, fill

Other Spellings for Root:
-pli- -plex-
-plic-

Examples:
ply, supplies, imply
application, replied, complex
complicated, implications

-spire-

Root Meaning:
breathe

Other Spellings for Root:
-spir-

Examples:
spirit, inspire, perspire
expired, transpiring, uninspiring
respiration, inspirational

-sist-

Root Meaning:
stand

Other Spellings for Root:
-sta- -stit- -sti-
-stant- -(x)ist-

Examples:
exist, resistance, insist
instant, constant, stationary
stability, desist

-sens-

Root Meaning:
feel, sense

Other Spellings for Root:
-sen- -sense-
-sent- -senti-

Examples:
sense, sensitive, sentiments
resent, consenting, presented
insensitivities, sentimentality

-pend-

Root Meaning:
hang, weigh, spend

Other Spellings for Root:
-pen- -pens-
-pense-

Examples:
depend, suspense, impending
dependent, pendant, pendulum
pensive, interdependency

GA1304

112

GA1304

-duce-

Root Meaning:
lead

Other Spellings for Root:
-duc-   -duct-

Examples:
duct, reduce, induct
conductor, produce, introduce
productions, educational

-miss-

Root Meaning:
send, let go

Other Spellings for Root:
-mitt-   -mit-
-mise-   -mis-

Examples:
admit, permission, omit
dismissal, committed, promising
demise, submitting

-tend-

Root Meaning:
stretch

Other Spellings for Root:
-ten-   -tens-
-tense-

Examples:
tense, intending, attended
pretends, extension, intense
unintentional, pretension

-fer-

Root Meaning:
carry, bear
bring meaning

Other Spellings for Root:
-ferr-   -fere-

Examples:
refer, offering, preferred
conference, transferring, inference
inferential, preferential

-cept-

Root Meaning:
take

Other Spellings for Root:
-ceive-

Examples:
accept, receive, deception
reception, intercepted, deceive
unacceptable, perceiving

-serve-

Root Meaning:
save, keep, serve

Other Spellings for Root:
-serv-

Examples:
serve, servant, preserves
conservation, reservation, disservice
subservient, unobservable

-vert-

Root Meaning:
turn

Other Spellings for Root:
-vers-   -verse-

Examples:
verse, revert, divert
inversion, reverse, perverse
convertible, subversive

-tain-

Root Meaning:
hold, keep

Other Spellings for Root:
-tent-   -tin-
-ten-

Examples:
contents, obtain, attention
intention, detain, pertinent
sustenance, retained

-cess-

Root Meaning:
go, give in

Other Spellings for Root:
-ced-   -ceed-
-cede-

Examples:
proceed, succeeds, recess
unsuccessful, access, concessions
processional, excessive

GA1304

114

GA1304

-fuse-

Root Meaning:
pour

Other Spellings for Root:
-fus-

Examples:
fuse, confusion, refusal
profusely, infusion, diffuser
transfusions, effusively

-gress-

Root Meaning:
step, go

Other Spellings for Root:
-gred-   -grad-
-grade-

Examples:
grade, gradual, progress
regression, ungraded, degrading
gradation, aggressively

-port-

Root Meaning:
carry

Examples:
port, transports, imported
porter, exports, portable
transportation, deportment

-form-

Root Meaning:
shape, furnish, act

Examples:
form, information, conforming
performances, deformed, informant
reformatory, transformations

-press-

Root Meaning:
hold, press

Examples:
press, impressed, depressed
pressure, expresses, compressing
unimpressionable, suppressed

WILD

You may use this
card for **ANY** single
prefix, root, or suffix
in the English
language!

CARD

-tract-

Root Meaning:
draw, pull

Examples:
tractor, subtracted, attracts
extracting, contract, detraction
protractor, unattractive

-ject-

Root Meaning:
throw

Examples:
reject, projects, injection
objections, subjects, eject
interjected, dejected

WILD

You may use this
card for **ANY** single
prefix, root, or suffix
in the English
language!

CARD

GA1304

116

GA1304

WILD

You may use this card for **ANY** single prefix, root, or suffix in the English language!

CARD

WILD

You may use this card for **ANY** single prefix, root, or suffix in the English language!

CARD

WILD

You may use this card for **ANY** single prefix, root, or suffix in the English language!

CARD

WILD

You may use this card for **ANY** single prefix, root, or suffix in the English language!

CARD

WILD

You may use this card for **ANY** single prefix, root, or suffix in the English language!

CARD

WILD

You may use this card for **ANY** single prefix, root, or suffix in the English language!

CARD

WILD

You may use this card for **ANY** single prefix, root, or suffix in the English language!

CARD

WILD

You may use this card for **ANY** single prefix, root, or suffix in the English language!

CARD

WILD

You may use this card for **ANY** single prefix, root, or suffix in the English language!

CARD

118

GA1304

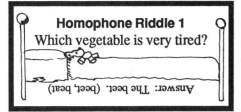

Homophone Riddle 1

Which vegetable is very tired?

Answer: The beet. (beet, beat)

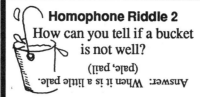

Homophone Riddle 2

How can you tell if a bucket is not well?

Answer: When it is a little pale. (pale, pail)

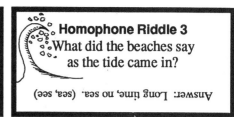

Homophone Riddle 3

What did the beaches say as the tide came in?

Answer: Long time, no sea. (sea, see)

Homophone Riddle 4

What did the dog say when he sat on the sandpaper?

Answer: Ruff, ruff, ruff! (ruff, rough)

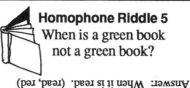

Homophone Riddle 5

When is a green book not a green book?

Answer: When it is read. (read, red)

Homophone Riddle 6

When is a store like a boat?

Answer: When it has sales. (sales, sails)

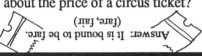

Homophone Riddle 7

Why should you never complain about the price of a circus ticket?

Answer: It is bound to be fair. (fare, fair)

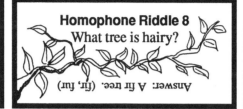

Homophone Riddle 8

What tree is hairy?

Answer: A fir tree. (fir, fur)

Homophone Riddle 9

What did the paper say to the pencil?

Answer: Write on! (write, right)

Homophone Riddle 10

Where do you put letters to boys?

Answer: In a mailbox. (male, mail)

Homophone Riddle 11

Why did the bald man buy a rabbit?

Answer: He wanted a head of hare. (hare, hair)

Homophone Riddle 12

What has a soul but can't be saved?

Answer: A shoe. (soul, sole)

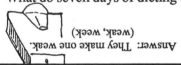

Homophone Riddle 13

What do seven days of dieting do?

Answer: They make one weak. (weak, week)

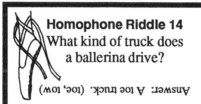

Homophone Riddle 14

What kind of truck does a ballerina drive?

Answer: A toe truck. (toe, tow)

Homophone Riddle 15

What do bees do with all of their honey?

Answer: They cell it. (cell, sell)

Homophone Riddle 16

What kind of school did the king run?

Answer: A knight school. (knight, night)

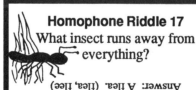

Homophone Riddle 17

What insect runs away from everything?

Answer: A flea. (flea, flee)

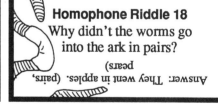

Homophone Riddle 18

Why didn't the worms go into the ark in pairs?

Answer: They went in apples. (pairs, pears)

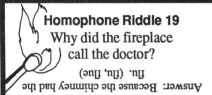

Homophone Riddle 19

Why did the fireplace call the doctor?

Answer: Because the chimney had the flu. (flu, flue)

Homophone Riddle 20

When does a horse suddenly become heavier?

Answer: When it is lead. (lead, led)

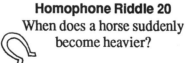

Homophone Riddle 21

What animal did the pig become when he caught a cold?

Answer: A little horse. (horse, hoarse)

Homophone Riddle 22

What team cries when it loses?

Answer: A bawl club. (bawl, ball)

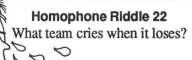

Homophone Riddle 23

What do you call a person who runs an ice cream truck?

Answer: A sundae driver. (sundae, Sunday)

Homophone Riddle 24

Why did the farmer take a needle into his fields?

Answer: To sow the corn. (sow, sew)

GA1304

Homophone Riddle 25
What dog has money?

Answer: A bloodhound, because he is always picking up scents. (scents, cents)

Homophone Riddle 26
What animal do you look like when you take a bath?

Answer: A little bear. (bear, bare)

Homophone Riddle 27
How long did Cain hate his brother?

Answer: As long as he was Abel. (Abel, able)

Homophone Riddle 28
How many relatives were at the family picnic?

Answer: Four uncles and 50,000 aunts. (aunts, ants)

Homophone Riddle 29
Where were the first French fries made?

Answer: In Greece. (Greece, grease)

Homophone Riddle 30
On what day of the year did soldiers start wars?

Answer: March fourth. (fourth, forth)

Homophone Riddle 31
When is a grown man still a child?

Answer: When he is a minor. (minor, miner)

Homophone Riddle 32
When is world unrest like a faulty jigsaw puzzle?

Answer: When a peace is missing. (peace, piece)

Homophone Riddle 33
Why should you never gossip in a stable?

Answer: Because all the horses carry tails. (tails, tales)

Homophone Riddle 34
What did the fat man say as he ate a large plate of food?

Answer: I'm afraid this is all going to waist. (waist, waste)

Homophone Riddle 35
What did the ear hear?

Answer: Only the nose knows. (nose, knows)

Homophone Riddle 36
What is the principal part of a horse?

Answer: The mane part. (mane, main)

Homophone Riddle 37
What is the correct thing to do before the King of Trees?

Answer: Bough. (Bough, bow)

Homophone Riddle 38
Why does a lion kneel before it springs?

Answer: Because it is preying. (preying, praying)

Homophone Riddle 39
What would you get if you crossed a doughnut with a pretzel?

Answer: You'd get a whole new twist. (whole, hole)

Homophone Riddle 40
Why are mountain climbers curious?

Answer: They always want to take another peak. (peak, peek)

Homophone Riddle 41
Why are fat men sad?

Answer: Because they are men of sighs. (sighs, size)

Homophone Riddle 42
Where does the sandman keep his sleeping sand?

Answer: In a napsack. (napsack, knapsack)

Homophone Riddle 43
What did the farmer do when he was arrested?

Answer: He posted bale. (bale, bail)

Homophone Riddle 44
Why do ships use knots instead of miles?

Answer: To keep the ocean tide. (tide, tied)

Homophone Riddle 45
Why is a rock braver than a mountain?

Answer: Because it is a little boulder. (boulder, bolder)

Homophone Riddle 46
What would happen if cows were put into orbit?

Answer: It would be the first herd shot around the world. (herd, heard)

Homophone Riddle 47
What is the difference between a pen and a pencil?

Answer: You push a pen but a pencil has to be led. (led, lead)

Homophone Riddle 48
Why is a well-trained horse like a kind-hearted person?

Answer: It always stops at the sound of woe. (woe, whoa)

GA1304

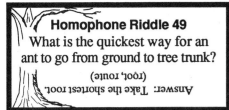

Homophone Riddle 49
What is the quickest way for an ant to go from ground to tree trunk?

Answer: Take the shortest root. (root, route)

Homophone Riddle 50
How do you hire a horse?

Answer: Put four bricks under it. (hire, higher)

Homophone Riddle 51
When are the golfers honest?

Answer: When they tell the hole truth. (hole, whole)

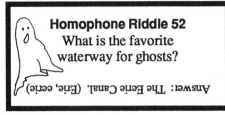

Homophone Riddle 52
What is the favorite waterway for ghosts?

Answer: The Eerie Canal. (Erie, eerie)

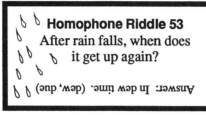

Homophone Riddle 53
After rain falls, when does it get up again?

Answer: In dew time. (dew, due)

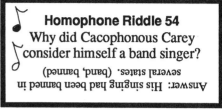

Homophone Riddle 54
Why did Cacophonous Carey consider himself a band singer?

Answer: His singing had been banned in several states. (band, banned)

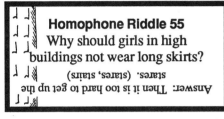

Homophone Riddle 55
Why should girls in high buildings not wear long skirts?

Answer: Then it is too hard to get up the stares. (stares, stairs)

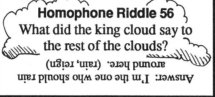

Homophone Riddle 56
What did the king cloud say to the rest of the clouds?

Answer: I'm the one who should rain around here. (rain, reign)

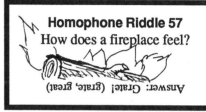

Homophone Riddle 57
How does a fireplace feel?

Answer: Grate! (grate, great)

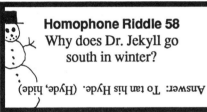

Homophone Riddle 58
Why does Dr. Jekyll go south in winter?

Answer: To tan his Hyde. (Hyde, hide)

Homophone Riddle 59
What happened after the little boy started bawling?

Answer: After four balls, he got his base warmed. (bawl, ball)

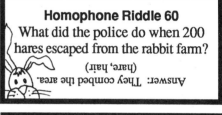

Homophone Riddle 60
What did the police do when 200 hares escaped from the rabbit farm?

Answer: They combed the area. (hare, hair)

Homophone Riddle 61
Why couldn't the church tower keep a secret?

Answer: The bell always tolled. (tolled, told)

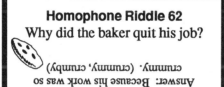

Homophone Riddle 62
Why did the baker quit his job?

Answer: Because his work was so crummy. (crummy, crumby)

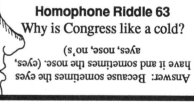

Homophone Riddle 63
Why is Congress like a cold?

Answer: Because sometimes the eyes have it and sometimes the nose. (eyes, ayes, nose, no's)

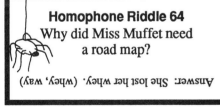

Homophone Riddle 64
Why did Miss Muffet need a road map?

Answer: She lost her whey. (whey, way)

Homophone Riddle 65
What do you get if you cross a banana and a comedian?

Answer: Peel of laughter. (peels, peals)

Homophone Riddle 66
What instrument of war does an angry lover resemble?

Answer: A crossbow. (bow, beau)

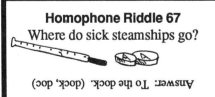

Homophone Riddle 67
Where do sick steamships go?

Answer: To the dock. (dock, doc)

Homophone Riddle 68
Why is a theater such a sad place?

Answer: Because the seats are in tiers. (tiers, tears)

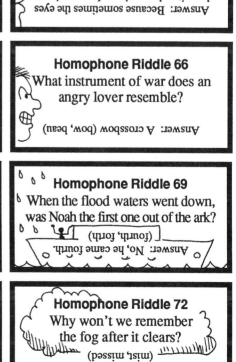

Homophone Riddle 69
When the flood waters went down, was Noah the first one out of the ark?

Answer: No, he came fourth. (fourth, forth)

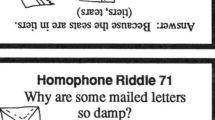

Homophone Riddle 70
What is the most confusing sign seen in a library?

Answer: To speak aloud is not allowed. (aloud, allowed)

Homophone Riddle 71
Why are some mailed letters so damp?

Answer: From the postage dew. (dew, due)

Homophone Riddle 72
Why won't we remember the fog after it clears?

Answer: Then it won't be mist. (mist, missed)

GA1304

Homophone Riddle 73
What musical instrument doesn't tell the truth?

Answer: A lyre. (lyre, liar)

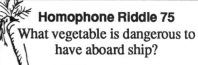

Homophone Riddle 74
What time is it when a knight looks at his belly button?

Answer: It is the middle of the night. (night, knight)

Homophone Riddle 75
What vegetable is dangerous to have aboard ship?

Answer: A leek. (leek, leak)

Homophone Riddle 76
Why are fencers so unpredictable?

Answer: Because of their dual personalities. (duel, dual)

Homophone Riddle 77
Where is a walking stick mentioned in the Bible?

Answer: Where Eve presented Adam with a little Cain. (Cain, cane)

Homophone Riddle 78
Why were the two red blood cells so unhappy?

Answer: They loved in vein. (vein, vain)

Homophone Riddle 79
What kind of insect likes to bowl?

Answer: The boll weevil. (bowl, boll)

Homophone Riddle 80
What people are like the end of a book?

Answer: The Finnish. (Finnish, finish)

Homophone Riddle 81
What kind of horse comes from Pennsylvania?

Answer: A filly. (filly, Philly)

Homophone Riddle 82
When prices are going up, what remains stationary?

Answer: Writing paper and envelopes. (stationary, stationery)

Homophone Riddle 83
Why didn't the little boy want to get his hair cut?

Answer: He thought it was sheer nonsense. (shear, sheer)

Homophone Riddle 84
Which high-strung people have educated themselves?

Answer: Those who are self-taut. (taut, taught)

Homophone Riddle 85
What does a braggart do in public?

Answer: He blows his knows. (knows, nose)

Homophone Riddle 86
On what food should prizefighters train?

Answer: Mussels. (mussels, muscles)

Homophone Riddle 87
Why do we never have a moment to call our own?

Answer: Because the minutes are not hours. (hours, ours)

Homophone Riddle 88
What was Joan of Arc made of?

Answer: Maid of Orleans. (made, maid)

Homophone Riddle 89
What happened when the jeep ran over a popcorn box in the army?

Answer: Two kernels were killed. (kernels, colonels)

Homophone Riddle 90
What do Indians raise that you can get lost in?

Answer: Maize. (maize, maze)

Homophone Riddle 91
Why is a spectator like a beehive?

Answer: Because a spectator is a beholder, and a bee-holder is a beehive. (beholder, bee-holder)

Homophone Riddle 92
What should a lifeguard's stand be called?

Answer: A naval observatory. (navel, naval)

Homophone Riddle 93
What was the biology lab's cloning project called?

Answer: Designer genes. (genes, jeans)

Homophone Riddle 94
Why did the king become rude when he gave up his castles?

Answer: Because he had lost his manors. (manors, manners)

Homophone Riddle 95
Why is a locomotive like a stick of gum?

Answer: One goes choo-choo and the other goes chew-chew. (choo, chew)

Homophone Riddle 96
What is the difference between a cat and a comma?

Answer: One has paws at the end of its claws, the other a pause at the end of its clause.

GA1304

Expression Riddle 1
What did one insect say to the other insect?

Answer: Stop bugging me.

Expression Riddle 2
What did the adding machine say to the bookkeeper?

Answer: You can count on me.

Expression Riddle 3
Why do people beat their clocks?

Answer: To kill time.

Expression Riddle 4
What did the rug say to the floor?

Answer: I've got you covered.

Expression Riddle 5
What happened when the chimney got angry?

Answer: It blew its stack.

Expression Riddle 6
What did one shrub say to the other shrub?

Answer: I am bushed!

Expression Riddle 7
When do clocks die?

Answer: When their time is up.

Expression Riddle 8
What did the tree say to the ax?

Answer: I'm stumped!

Expression Riddle 9
Why are garbage men unhappy?

Answer: Because they are down in the dumps so much.

Expression Riddle 10
What did one faucet say to the other faucet?

Answer: You're just a big drip.

Expression Riddle 11
When is a clock nervous?

Answer: When it is all wound up.

Expression Riddle 12
Why shouldn't you tell a joke while you are ice skating?

Answer: Because the ice might crack up.

Expression Riddle 13
Why did the hippie like to stand in front of the electric fan?

Answer: It blew his mind.

Expression Riddle 14
What happened to the couple who met in a revolving door?

Answer: They're still going around together.

Expression Riddle 15
Why did the pretty school teacher marry the janitor?

Answer: Because he swept her off her feet.

Expression Riddle 16
Why did the mother ghost take her child to the doctor?

Answer: She was worried because he was in such good spirits.

Expression Riddle 17
Why did the orchestra have bad manners?

Answer: Because it didn't know how to conduct itself.

Expression Riddle 18
Why was the mother flea so sad?

Answer: Because her children were going to the dogs.

Expression Riddle 19
Why are mosquitoes so bothersome?

Answer: Because they get under your skin.

Expression Riddle 20
What advice can you give a fish so he can avoid being caught?

Answer: Don't fall for any old line.

Expression Riddle 21
What is the quietest sport?

Answer: Bowling, because you can hear a pin drop.

Expression Riddle 22
Why shouldn't you tell secrets when a clock is around?

Answer: Because time will tell.

Expression Riddle 23
Why couldn't Humpty Dumpty be put together again?

Answer: Because he wasn't everything he was cracked up to be.

Expression Riddle 24
Why did the man have to fix the horn on his car?

Answer: Because it didn't give a hoot.

Expression Riddle 25
When does a caterpillar improve in behavior?

Answer: When it turns over a new leaf.

Expression Riddle 26
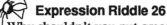
Why shouldn't you put grease on your hair the night before a test?

Answer: If you did, everything might slip your mind.

Expression Riddle 27
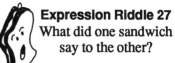
What did one sandwich say to the other?

Answer: You're full of bologna.

Expression Riddle 28
Why didn't the man tell the joke about the green germ?

Answer: Because he didn't want to spread it around.

Expression Riddle 29
What did the leopard say when it started to rain?

Answer: That hits the spots.

Expression Riddle 30
What did one owl say to the other owl?

Answer: I don't give a hoot about you.

Expression Riddle 31
Why was the little strawberry worried?

Answer: Because his mom and dad were in a jam.

Expression Riddle 32
Why did the man take a bag of oats with him when he took his girlfriend out to dinner?

Answer: Because she ate like a horse.

Expression Riddle 33
Why didn't the boy understand the joke about the roof?

Answer: It was over his head.

Expression Riddle 34
What one quality should a worm look for most in a friend?

Answer: One who is down-to-earth.

Expression Riddle 35
Why did the man name his pig "Ballpoint"?

Answer: He wanted his pig to have a pen name.

Expression Riddle 36
What is a minister doing when he rehearses his sermons?

Answer: He is practicing what he preaches.

Expression Riddle 37
Why did the angry man go to a tailor?

Answer: So he could have a fit.

Expression Riddle 38
Why are dogs such terrible dancers?

Answer: Because they all have two left feet.

Expression Riddle 39
What did one elevator say to the other elevator?

Answer: I think I'm coming down with something.

Expression Riddle 40
What would happen if you ate yeast and polish?

Answer: You would rise and shine.

Expression Riddle 41
Why can't people talk while goats are around?

Answer: Because the goats always butt in.

Expression Riddle 42
What did the dirt say to the rain?

Answer: If this keeps up, my name will be mud.

Expression Riddle 43
Why did the man keep a ruler on his newspaper?

Answer: Because he wanted to get the story straight.

Expression Riddle 44
What did the wig say to the head?

Answer: I've got you covered.

Expression Riddle 45
What do people do in a clock factory?

Answer: They make faces all day.

Expression Riddle 46
What would you get if you crossed a skunk and an eagle?

Answer: An animal that stunk to high heaven.

Expression Riddle 47

What did people say when the man got out of his rocking chair after twenty years?

Answer: He must be off his rocker.

Expression Riddle 48
Why did the invisible man go crazy?

Answer: Out of sight, out of mind.

GA1304

Expression Riddle 49
When are people like eyeglasses?

Answer: When they make spectacles of themselves.

Expression Riddle 50
Why did the astronomer hit himself on the head each afternoon?

Answer: Because he wanted to see stars during the day.

Expression Riddle 51
What is the best way to communicate with a fish?

Answer: Drop him a line.

Expression Riddle 52
Why are birds poor?

Answer: Because money doesn't grow on trees.

Expression Riddle 53
Why did the girl sit on her watch?

Answer: Because she wanted to be on time.

Expression Riddle 54
Why couldn't the mummy answer the telephone?

Answer: Because he was all tied up.

Expression Riddle 55
Why should you stay calm when you meet a cannibal?

Answer: Because you don't want to get into a stew.

Expression Riddle 56
Who invented spaghetti?

Answer: Someone who used his noodle.

Expression Riddle 57
Why would someone in jail want to catch the measles?

Answer: So he could break out.

Expression Riddle 58
What did the skunk say when the wind changed?

Answer: It all comes back to me now.

Expression Riddle 59
Why did the man put iodine on his paycheck?

Answer: Because he got a cut in his salary.

Expression Riddle 60
Why did the man sit in front of the electric fan with a BB gun?

Answer: Because he wanted to shoot the breeze.

Expression Riddle 61
Why did the two boa constrictors get married?

Answer: Because they had a crush on each other.

Expression Riddle 62
What happened to the pianist whose hands were tied behind his back?

Answer: He played by ear.

Expression Riddle 63
Why did the laundry man declare bankruptcy?

Answer: Because he was all washed up.

Expression Riddle 64
What does a worm do in a cornfield?

Answer: It goes in one ear and out another.

Expression Riddle 65
Why don't cows ever have any money?

Answer: Because the farmers are always milking them dry.

Expression Riddle 66
Why do dentists seem moody?

Answer: Because they always look down in the mouth.

Expression Riddle 67
What is the loudest sport?

Answer: Tennis, because everyone is raising a racquet (racket).

Expression Riddle 68
Why don't flies fly through screen doors?

Answer: Because they don't want to strain themselves.

Expression Riddle 69
Who has the strongest fingers in the world?

Answer: A miser, because he is always pinching pennies.

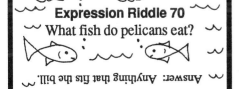

Expression Riddle 70
What fish do pelicans eat?

Answer: Anything that fits the bill.

Expression Riddle 71
What happens to a refrigerator when you pull its plug?

Answer: It loses its cool.

Expression Riddle 72
Why don't scarecrows have any fun?

Answer: Because they are stuffed shirts.

Expression Riddle 73
Why do gardeners hate weeds?

Answer: Give weeds an inch and they'll take a yard.

Expression Riddle 74
Why did the farmer plant sugar cubes?

Answer: Because he wanted to raise cane.

Expression Riddle 75
Why was the Marine sergeant discharged?

Answer: Because he was rotten to the Corps.

Expression Riddle 76
What animals are the cheapest to feed?

Answer: Giraffes, because they make a little food go a long way.

Expression Riddle 77
Who gets fed up with people?

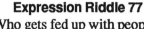

Answer: A cannibal.

Expression Riddle 78
Why didn't the man lend his friend a dollar?

Answer: Because he didn't believe in passing the buck.

Expression Riddle 79
Why was the farmer angry?

Answer: Because someone got his goat.

Expression Riddle 80
Why did the two history students get together?

Answer: So they could talk over old times.

Expression Riddle 81
What should you do if you were carried out to sea on an iceberg?

Answer: Keep cool until rescued.

Expression Riddle 82
Why did the knife sharpener quit his job?

Answer: It was too much of a grind.

Expression Riddle 83
Why can you always believe a ruler?

Answer: Because it is on the level.

Expression Riddle 84
Why did the chicken go just halfway across the road?

Answer: Because she wanted to lay it on the line.

Expression Riddle 85
What did the frankfurter say when the dog bit him?

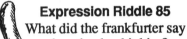

Answer: It's a dog-eat-dog world.

Expression Riddle 86
Why did the wife understand her invisible husband so well?

Answer: Because she could see right through him

Expression Riddle 87
What are the most faithful insects?

Answer: Ticks, because once they find friends, they stick to them.

Expression Riddle 88
Why is the snake the smartest animal in the world?

Answer: Because no one can pull its leg.

Expression Riddle 89
Why did the girl tear the calendar?

Answer: Because she wanted to take a month off.

Expression Riddle 90
What happened to the guy who stole the calendar?

Answer: He got twelve months.

Expression Riddle 91
Why was the woman ironing her four-leaf clover?

Answer: Because she was pressing her luck.

Expression Riddle 92
Why did the midget lack self-confidence?

Answer: Because he always sold himself short.

Expression Riddle 93
When is a leaky faucet like a racehorse?

Answer: When it is off and running.

Expression Riddle 94
What did the father tree say to his son?

Answer: You're a chip off the old block.

Expression Riddle 95
When is a hat not a hat?

Answer: When it becomes a girl.

Expression Riddle 96
What did Mason say to Dixon?

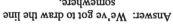

Answer: We've got to draw the line somewhere.

GA1304

accused, acknowledged, added, addressed, adduced, admitted, advised, advocated, affirmed, agreed, alleged, allowed, announced, answered, antagonized, apologized, appealed, applauded, apprised, argued, articulated, asked, asserted, assured, averred, avowed, babbled, badgered, bantered, barked, bawled, bayed, beckoned, began, begged, belched, believed, belittled, bellowed, bemoaned, beseeched, bewailed, bickered, blubbered, bluffed, blundered, blurted out, blustered, boasted, boomed, bragged, broadcasted, brooded, bubbled, burped, butted in, buzzed, cajoled, called, cautioned, challenged, chanted, charged, chatted, chattered, cheered, chided, chimed in, chirped, choked, chuckled, cited

"Said" Is Dead: A Synonym Activity

Many words are frequently overused in writing or speaking. Some examples are **said, nice, great, neat,** or **wild.** The following passage originally contained the word **said** in each blank. After examining the words shown in the borders of this page, write a different substitute for **said** in each blank space. In your future writing and speaking, try to use many of these words.

"Gang Gong's Dilemma"

"Quiet, everyone!" _____ Shawn, the gang's president. "We must decide about the new boy who just moved into our subdivision today. Do you think we should invite him to join 'Gang Gong'?"

"We haven't even met him yet," Jerry _____. "Does anybody know anything about him?"

"His name is Chris," _____ Bill. "Chris Hardin. That is all I know."

"Wait, boys," Smally _____. "I think--"

"And he's thirteen, like all of us," Bucky _____. "I heard Granny Hyder tell Mom that all we needed was another teenager in the neighborhood."

"Do we have to decide tonight?" Walter _____. "If we wait until tomorrow, we can find out more about him at school."

"However," Jim _____, "if we wait, then 'Gang Green' might ask him to join their club first."

"That's right," Jerry _____. "They already have twelve members. That's four more than we have."

"But," _____ Smally, "we can't--"

"I vote for inviting Chris to join tonight," _____ Tommy. "After we collect his entrance fee, we can kick him out if we don't like him."

"I tell you," Smally _____, "Chris is--"

"Yes, we'll kick him out if we don't like him," Bucky _____. "Maybe we should do that to someone now."

They all turned and stared at Smally. Yesterday Smally angered them by admitting to the teacher who had poured the molasses on the gymnasium floor. Betraying one's "Gang Gong" brother carried a stiff penalty. Smally knew he must remain silent for the rest of the evening.

A noise interrupted their meeting. Through the fence the boys could see the Hardin's back door open. Out stepped Chris.

"Sh-h-h, there he is," _____ Jerry.

"You are right," _____ Bill. "Let's see what he looks like."

"What funny-looking yellow pants!" Walter _____.

"Oh, no!" Frank _____. "Look at him walk."

"Why don't we go over and talk to him?" _____ Bucky. "Then if we don't like him, we won't ask him to join."

"Good idea," Bill _____.

"Let's go," Jim _____.

Seven boys raced to the Hardin's house. Only Smally remained. He knew Chris was a girl.

harped on, hedged, heralded, hinted, hissed, howled, hypothesized, idolized, intimated, implied, implored, indicated, inferred, informed, inquired, inserted, insinuated, insisted, instructed, interjected, interpreted, interrogated, interrupted, intimidated, intoned, intonated, invited, iterated, jeered, jested, joined in, joked, joshed, kidded, lamented, lashed out, laughed, lied, lisped, maintained, mentioned, meowed, mewed, mimicked, mispronounced, misquoted, moaned, mocked, mourned, mumbled, murmured, mused, muttered, nagged, named, narrated, nixed, noted, objected, observed, opined, ordered, outlined, panted, paraphrased, persisted, persuaded, petitioned, piped, pleaded, pointed out, pouted halt, advance; brave, cowardly; countryman, townsman; frequently, seldom; meager, abundant; voluntary, compulsory helpful, useless; restrain, yield; daughter, son; absent, present; same, different; add, subtract; cruel, kind; friend, enemy evening, morning; day, night; wild, tame; yesterday, tomorrow; best, worst; pass, fail; war, peace; Mom, Dad; wet, dry cool, warm; dry, moist; gain, loss; soft, loud; hero, coward; common, odd; aid, oppose; for, against; bold, timid

Zany Antonyms

Why do we say "our forefathers" instead of "our foremothers"? If we changed some of our male-sounding words to their female counterparts (or vice versa), we could create some zany antonyms. Complete the exercise below by first determining the serious word which is defined on the left side of the page. Then determine its newly created zany antonym on the right. After completing this exercise, see if you can create some new zany opposites for a fun time with your friends.

A printed list of foods which may be ordered in a restaurant

A printed list of foods which only adult females may order in a restaurant

Word: _____

Zany antonym: _____

The capital of Idaho

A city where young females live

Word: _____

Zany antonym: _____

A tropical cyclone with fierce winds, usually accompanied by rain, thunder, and lightning

A walking stick for males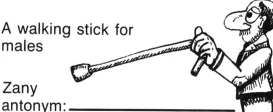

Word: _____

Zany antonym: _____

To join other persons in having no dealings with a certain person, business, or organization

A small collapsible bed for young females

Word: _____

Zany antonym: _____

A command; an order, especially a formal order from a superior court; an obligation

An adult female who has a social engagement with a male

Word: _____

Zany antonym: _____

evil, good; witty, dull; sharp, dull; multiply, divide; constant, variable; vain, modest; usual, rare; vacant, occupied joy, grief; unite, divide; male, female; positive, negative; prompt, tardy; punish, reward; whole, part; stern, gentle accelerate, decelerate; migrate, settle; increase, decrease; forward, backward; afraid, fearless; abundant, scarce question, answer; fat, skinny; first, last; something, nothing; blond, brunette; famous, unknown; playful, serious

profit, loss; vertical, horizontal; maximum, minimum; bless, curse; complex, simple; inferior, superior; convex, concave; create, destroy; reject, accept; passive, active naive, sophisticated; discord, harmony; expand, contract; abstract, concrete; gradual, sudden; diminish, increase; outward, inward; faithful, fickle; fact, fiction; won, lost compliment, insult; conceal, reveal; applicable, irrelevant; worldly, heavenly; normal, abnormal; firm, flabby; nephew, niece; coarse, fine; enormous, tiny; in, out guilty, innocent; logical, illogical; retard, accelerate; remain, depart; synonym, antonym; honorable, dishonorable; behave, misbehave; objective, subjective; yes, no

commence, finalize; decent, indecent, punctual, late; expressive, receptive; lengthen, shorten; introvert, extrovert; barbarian, civilized lavish, sparing; blatant, reserved; belligerent, friendly; clandestine, open; incarcerated, free; homogeneous, heterogeneous; euphony, cacophony; same, different remember, forget; absent, present; lengthen, shorten; sober, drunk; work, play; praise, blame; careful, careless; heal, wound; never, always; hello, _____ off, on connect, separate; succeed, fail; aunt, uncle; rise, fall; smooth, rough; asleep, awake; sloppy, neat; care, neglect; help, hinder; head, tail; humble, proud; devil, angel

GA1304

Who's Afraid of Phobophobiacs?

Who is a phobophobiac? If you recognize the root word *phobia* as meaning "fear," then you will know that a phobophobiac is one who is afraid of being afraid. Below are six words which may be new to you. These are words for people who have intense fears. Study the words carefully and write them in the blank spaces by their corresponding drawings.

**Zoophobiac, Bibliophobiac, Claustrophobiac,
Thermophobiac, Meteorophobiac, Vaccinophobiac**

1._____

2._____

3._____

4._____

5._____

6._____

GA1304

Eponyms for Vocabulary Fun

Synonyms, antonyms and homonyms are terms which are commonly used in vocabulary study. But what are **eponyms?**

A person (or place) whose name becomes a new and common word is called an eponym (pronounced \\' ep-uh-' nim\\). The person might soon be forgotten, but the new word becomes a part of everyday vocabulary.

An example is the word **sandwich.** This became a common word because of a British Earl of Sandwich who played cards continuously. He did not wish to stop for a meal, and neither did he want to get his fingers messy by touching the food which was brought to him. Therefore he ordered a servant to wrap bread around his meat. In this manner he could eat without stopping his card playing and without messing his fingers. Soon others began eating food in this same manner and **sandwich** became a common word.

Not all eponyms are from names of people. Some are from the places where an idea or product first became popular.

The blanks in the following passages are both the product and the name of the person (or place) that made the product well-known. How many of them do you know? (The first letters are provided.)

Ebenezer S_____ was a character in one of Charles Dickens' novels. Until the end of the story he was a mean and stingy tightwad. A person today who is both mean and stingy (especially near Christmas) is often called s_____ .

Jules L_____ was a French circus performer who was uncomfortable in regular clothes when he performed. He had tailors prepare a one-piece bodysuit which would cling snugly to his skin. Today many such performers and exercisers frequently wear a garment called l_____s.

Nellie M_____ was a famous opera singer who was always on a diet. Once she asked that her toast be cut extra thin so there would be fewer calories per serving. A cook accidentally left it in the oven too long, causing the toast to become very brown. However, she liked the taste. Others liked it also, and soon the restaurant boasted of a new menu item: m_____ toast.

A few years ago some of the drivers for the F_____ Pie Company became bored during their lunch breaks. They started tossing the tin pie plates to each other. Soon others began a similar activity. Shortly afterwards a plastic throwing disk which was called a F_____® was manufactured and named after the pie company.

Pretend that **your name** (either first or last) will become an eponym in the future because of something you will invent or a new idea which you will cause to become popular. Write an explanation of your new product or idea. Include in this explanation the impact this new trend will have on society.

_____

_____

_____

_____

_____

_____

GA1304

Those Crazy Idioms

Sometimes the comprehension of a phrase or sentence is *not* the collective interpretation of its individual words. The English language is filled with special or unique phrases which have meaning *as word **groups** only*. The **idiom** is one of these types of word groups. Below and on the following page several idioms are illustrated, each with two different drawings. One drawing shows the correct interpretation of the idiom. The other shows its incorrect (or literal) interpretation. Choose the drawing which represents the correct meaning.

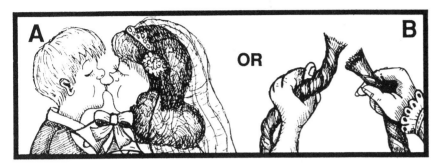

1.
George and Jennifer tied the knot. ⇐

2.
Frank and Tom finally buried the hatchet. ⇒

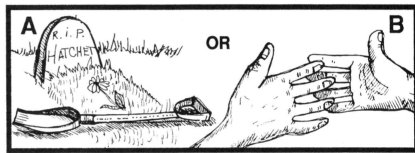

3.
After they won the lottery, the Clarks ate high on the hog. ⇐

4.
William lost face after he failed to keep his promise. ⇒

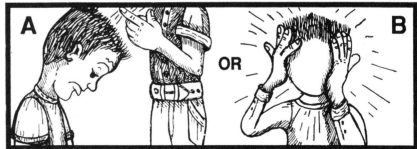

5.
The judge threw the book at Denise after her fourth appearance in court. ⇐

GA1304

6.
⇐ Jimmy's father is a
big wheel.

7.
After the disagreement,
Ellen gave Susan the ⇒
cold shoulder.

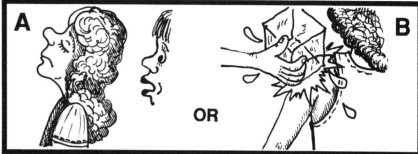

8.
Jane knew her mother
wanted a new coat for
⇐ her birthday, so she put
a bug in her father's ear.

9.
When Mary heard of the
vacation plans, she was ⇒
on cloud nine.

10.
⇐ By the end of the evening,
Jason's baby-sitter was
climbing the wall.

11.
When John heard the
money was missing, he ⇒
smelled a rat.

GA1304

LISTS,
ANSWERS,
AND
CONTAINERS

(Note: The design on the back of this page and on pages 4, 6, 12, and 14 are offered as alternatives to the backs of the Worbic deck of playing cards.)

A Partial List of Synonyms

Note: This list of synonyms is provided for instructors to use in preparing synonym games and activities. Some difficulty exists with any attempt to compile a list of synonyms. By their very nature, synonyms have similar, not exact, meanings. Therefore, a learner might respond, "Turn and spin do not mean the same thing." They do not have the same meaning, but in many contexts, their meanings are very similar. Please use your own judgment regarding which pairs of synonyms to select for any teaching situation. In some cases, the reader might need to know the part of speech of one of the words in the pair, such as free and release. Also, homographs may possibly present some difficulty for the reader. Such an example would be refuse. When pronounced \ri-ˈfyüz\, it has a synonym of deny; however, when pronounced \ˈref-yüs\, a synonym might be trash or garbage. Words such as these may prompt needed discussions of other areas of vocabulary study. This list is presented from easy to difficult pairs.

big, large	also, too	false, wrong	fall, decline	rise, ascend
tiny, little	beautiful, pretty	swell, expand	usual, ordinary	discrimination,
fat, heavy	cafeteria, lunchroom	law, rule	celestial, heavenly	discernment
mad, angry	hurt, injure	order, arrangement	trial, test	respect, regard
near, close	lift, raise	stingy, tight	error, mistake	restrain, repress
old, aged	messy, untidy	keep, preserve	bad, evil	representative, agent
act, play	needed, necessary	attach, fasten	try, attempt	scatter, disperse
dog, mutt	gather, collect	careful, cautious	fact, truth	worth, value
cat, kitty	robber, thief	cop, policeman	false, untruth	prejudice, bias
cart, wagon	chair, seat	blink, wink	funny, humorous	presume, suppose
happy, glad	plate, dish	growl, snarl	previous, prior	predict, prophecy
brag, boast	trip, journey	deck, pack	proper, right	ingredient, component
jump, hop	bad, wicked	clean, spotless	honest, sincere	rival, competitor
rip, tear	light, lamp	woods, forest	frank, candid	creditable, respectable
fast, quick	luggage, baggage	open, public	hinder, prevent	savage, uncivilized
hobble, limp	shy, bashful	fix, repair	humble, meek	anxiety, apprehension
sick, ill	strong, mighty	ship, boat	liquid, fluid	apparent, obvious
boil, cook	able, competent	house, home	lawful, legal	atrocious, monstrous
man, guy	many, numerous	quick, swift	pull, drag	accumulate, collect
woman, lady	taxi, cab	ready, alert	model, sample	review, resurvey
shut, close	all, every	clothing, robe	defer, delay	expensive, costly
joy, gladness	aid, help	plain, homely	real, actual	clippers, shears
letter, note	call, phone	path, trail	pet, favorite	luscious, delicious
mama, mother	about, near	free, release	start, beginning	people, persons
daddy, father	nice, polite	profit, gain	anger, rage	individuality,
fear, fright	hello, aloha	hard, harsh	girl, lass	distinctiveness
present, gift	after, behind	sure, certain	boy, lad	thicken, solidify
pot, kettle	good-bye, farewell	dodge, avoid	stop, halt	interval, span
story, tale	girl, gal	abandon, leave	part, portion	transparent, clear
reason, cause	baby, infant	hate, despise	method, system	constant, fixed
turn, spin	fire, blaze	abnormal, unusual	plea, request	stiff, rigid
above, over	flower, blossom	destroy, obliterate	plot, scheme	accomplish, achieve
ask, question	conclude, end	hasten, quicken	peace, tranquility	puzzle, perplex
right, correct	preceding, before	accident, calamity	first, primary	provoke, irritate
hold, grasp	following, after	amnesty, pardon	often, frequently	wretched, miserable
push, shove	calm, smooth	amazement, awe	royal, regal	toil, labor
long, endless	pain, agony	anonymous, nameless	oath, covenant	vivacious, lively
calm, quiet	suit, fit	answer, reply	protect, defend	superior, excellent
sadness, grief	oppose, resist	shape, mold	pupil, student	antique, archaic
huge, large	alive, living	brave, courageous	tardy, late	pure, clean
odd, strange	aim, goal	gentle, mild	proxy, substitution	pretend, allege
narrow, thin	similar, alike	authentic, genuine	refuse, deny	cloak, coat
begin, start	safe, unhurt	pursue, chase	road, street	obscene, indecent
safe, secure	hint, suggest	final, last	promise, pledge	purpose, intent
wide, broad	loud, noisy	assist, help	remain, stay	principle, rule
meadow, pasture	mend, repair	artificial, false	single, one	weakened,
same, alike	spoil, ruin	enough, sufficient	special, extraordinary	degenerated
scent, odor	cure, remedy	conceal, hide	lane, path	vindictive, revengeful

A Partial List of Synonyms for *Said*

*Note: Particular words in the speaking and writing vocabularies of young learners seem to be used repeatedly. These words should have planned practices and experiences with their synonyms. The exercise entitled "'Said' Is Dead: A Synonym Activity" (found elsewhere in this book) is such an example. This activity has many of the words listed below in small type as a border for the purpose of giving writers many choices for the blank spaces. These words were collected and compiled by a group of young learners who realized they relied upon the word **said** when other synonyms might communicate better.*

*After examining such a list, learners might select other words which they overuse and prepare a list of synonyms for those words. An activity which works well with students is to identify one such word each week. During the first two days the list of synonyms is prepared. For the entire week, no one may use the original word. A synonym **must** be substituted in all cases. For example, when the word for the week is **said**, no one can utter that word for seven days. If you think this is easy, **try it!***

Other such activities may also be developed to fulfill the goal of synonym substitutions.

The list below is presented alphabetically rather than in order of difficulty. Those words which relate to the needs of the learners involved may be extracted and presented. However, do not underestimate the knowledge base of the students or their ability to use dictionaries or a thesaurus to find new words.

accused	bluffed	confused	entreated	implied
acknowledged	blundered	congratulated	enumerated	implored
added	blurted out	consented	estimated	indicated
addressed	blustered	contended	eulogized	insinuated
adduced	boasted	continued	explained	insisted
admitted	boomed	contributed	exploded	instructed
advised	bragged	cooed	expounded	interjected
advocated	broadcasted	corrected	expressed	interpreted
affirmed	brooded	coughed	fabricated	interrogated
agreed	bubbled	counted	fibbed	interrupted
alleged	burped	cracked	filled in	intimidated
allowed	butted in	cried (out)	finished	intoned
announced	buzzed	criticized	fired	intonated
answered	cajoled	croaked	flattered	invited
antagonized	called	cross-examined	fretted	iterated
apologized	cautioned	crowed	fumed	jeered
appealed	challenged	cursed	fussed	jested
applauded	chanted	cussed	grabbed	joined (in)
apprised	charged	debated	grasped	joked
argued	chatted	decided	gawked	joshed
articulated	chattered	declaimed	gibed	kidded
asked	cheered	declared	giggled	lamented
asserted	chided	defined	gloated	lashed out
assured	chimed (in)	demanded	goaded	laughed
averred	chirped	demonstrated	gossiped	lied
avowed	choked	denied	grieved	lisped
babbled	chuckled	described	groaned	maintained
badgered	cited	dictated	growled	mentioned
bantered	claimed	directed	grumbled	meowed
barked	clamored	disagreed	grunted	mewed
bawled	clarified	discerned	guessed	mimicked
bayed	clucked	disclosed	gulped	mispronounced
beckoned	coaxed	disputed	gurgled	misquoted
began	commanded	divulged	hacked	moaned
begged	commenced	drawled	hammered	mocked
belched	commended	dreamed	harped	mourned
believed	commented	droned	hedged	mumbled
belittled	communicated	drummed	heralded	murmured
bellowed	complained	echoed	hinted	mused
bemoaned	complied	eluded	hissed	muttered
beseeched	complimented	emitted	howled	nagged
bewailed	concluded	emphasized	hypothesized	named
bickered	confessed	ended	idolized	narrated
blubbered	confirmed	enunciated	intimated	nixed

GA1304

noted	puffed	remembered	shuddered	talked
objected	purported	reminded	sighed	taunted
observed	purposed	reminisced	smarted off	teased
opined	purred	renounced	snapped	threatened
ordered	quacked	repeated	snored	thundered
outlined	quarrelled	replied	snorted	told
panted	queried	reported	sounded out	trumpeted
paraphrased	questioned	requested	spat	urged
persisted	quibbled	resounded	specified	uttered
persuaded	quipped	responded	speculated	ventured
petitioned	quizzed	restated	spit out	verbalized
piped	quoted	resumed	spoke	verified
pleaded	raged	retorted	sputtered	vocalized
pointed out	rasped	retracted	squawked	vowed
pouted	ratified	returned to	squeaked	wailed
praised	read	revealed	squealed	warbled
prayed	reasoned	reviewed	stammered	warned
preached	recalled	ridiculed	stated	whimpered
presented	recapitulated	roared	stormed	whined
presumed	recited	rumored	stressed	whispered
pretended	recommended	sang	stumbled	whistled
prevaricated	recounted	scoffed	stuttered	whizzed
proclaimed	reflected	scolded	suggested	wished
prodded	rehashed	scorned	sulked	witnessed
promised	rehearsed	screamed	summarized	wondered
prompted	reiterated	screeched	summed up	wooed
pronounced	rejoiced	shouted	summoned	wrangled
proposed	related	shrieked	surmised	yelled
protested	remarked	shrugged	swore	yelped

A Partial List of Antonyms

Note: This list of antonyms may provide some pairs of words to which learners may respond in games and activities designed to build this specific vocabulary subskill. It is important to remember that antonyms are words which have opposite or near opposite meanings. For example, doctor and nurse are not true opposites; however, they are often included in lists of antonym pairs. Discussions of these types of opposites may occur as additional information regarding language development.

The following list begins with words which are easier and more commonly used by young learners. It progresses in difficulty to some harder pairs of antonyms. Select those which fit the needs of the learners involved. Allow them to add to a prepared list as they encounter new sets of antonyms.

yes, no	strong, weak	deep, shallow	witty, dull	beginning, finale
in, out	laugh, cry	entrance, exit	sharp, dull	naive, sophisticated
black, white	love, hate	ahead, behind	multiply, divide	discord, harmony
up, down	raw, cooked	ask, tell	constant, variable	expand, contract
wet, dry	after, before	try, quit	vain, modest	abstract, concrete
hot, cold	pretty, ugly	wise, ignorant	usual, rare	gradual, sudden
off, on	narrow, wide	use, waste	vacant, occupied	diminish, increase
boy, girl	dead, alive	float, sink	joy, grief	outward, inward
front, back	young, old	fresh, stale	unite, divide	introduction,
win, lose	brother, sister	polite, rude	male, female	conclusion
easy, hard	empty, full	break, mend	positive, negative	faithful, fickle
good, bad	lost, found	sold, bought	prompt, tardy	fact, fiction
stop, go	sick, well	many, few	punish, reward	compliment, insult
top, bottom	daughter, son	plain, fancy	whole, part	conceal, reveal
high, low	absent, present	pitch, catch	stern, gentle	applicable, irrelevant
dark, light	same, different	sleep, awaken	accelerate, decelerate	worldly, heavenly
first, last	add, subtract	came, went	migrate, settle	normal, abnormal
fast, slow	cruel, kind	goose, gander	increase, decrease	firm, flabby
happy, sad	friend, enemy	whisper, yell	forward, backward	nephew, niece
man, woman	evening, morning	sit, stand	afraid, fearless	coarse, fine
early, late	day, night	give, take	abundant, scarce	enormous, tiny
sweet, sour	wild, tame	lend, borrow	question, answer	guilty, innocent
shut, open	yesterday, tomorrow	here, there	fat, skinny	logical, illogical
near, far	best, worst	crooked, straight	first, last	retard, accelerate
heavy, light	pass, fail	push, pull	something, nothing	remain, depart
come, go	war, peace	save, spend	blond, brunette	synonym, antonym
east, west	mom, dad	remember, forget	famous, unknown	honorable,
north, south	cool, warm	leader, follower	playful, serious	dishonorable
glad, sad	dry, moist	lengthen, shorten	halt, advance	behave, misbehave
fat, thin	gain, loss	work, play	brave, cowardly	objective, subjective
day, night	soft, loud	praise, blame	countryman,	decent, indecent
won, lost	hero, coward	careful, careless	townsman	punctual, late
live, die	common, odd	heal, wound	frequently, seldom	expressive, receptive
king, queen	aid, oppose	never, always	meager, abundant	lengthen, shorten
lad, lass	for, against	hello, good-bye	voluntary, compulsory	profitable,
lead, follow	bold, timid	connect, separate	helpful, useless	nonprofitable
short, tall	age, youth	succeed, fail	restrain, yield	commence, finalize
right, wrong	small, large	aunt, uncle	profit, loss	introvert, extrovert
big, little	friend, foe	rise, fall	vertical, horizontal	barbarian, civilized
great, small	victory, defeat	smooth, rough	maximum, minimum	lavish, sparing
more, less	cheap, expensive	asleep, awake	bless, curse	blatant, reserved
sell, buy	death, birth	sloppy, neat	complex, simple	belligerent, friendly
poor, rich	safe, dangerous	care, neglect	inferior, superior	clandestine, open
above, below	public, private	help, hinder	convex, concave	incarcerated, free
work, play	better, worse	head, tail	create, destroy	homogeneous,
begin, end	sickness, health	humble, proud	reject, accept	heterogeneous
false, true	agree, differ	evil, holy	passive, active	euphony, cacophony

GA1304

A Partial List of Homophones

*Note: This list of homophones may be used to provide the instructor with words for games and activities involving this vocabulary subskill. This list is by no means inclusive of the possibile sets of homophones which exist in the dialects of English-speaking people. Because of the vast differences in idiolects and dialects in America, an exhaustive list could not be prepared. This list, however, attempts to provide some "starters" for group activities. Some problems arose, however, even in the preparation and compilation of a starter list. A pair of words which are homophonous in one dialect might **not** be in another. An example is **pin** and **pen**. Those with a native Appalachian dialect might pronounce these two words as homophones. In other major dialects in the nation, these two words would have different medial vowel utterances. Many similar dialect differences exist. For example, the words **caught** and **cot** are homophonous in some areas, while others pronounce a very distinctly different vowel sound. All such phonemic substitutions in these dialects cannot be listed in a text such as this. A user of this list, however, should understand its limitations.*

*Another difficulty involves words with multiple acceptable pronunciations. The word **buoy** has two distinctly different pronunciations offered in most dictionaries—one which is homophonic with **boy**. Therefore, the words **buoy** and **boy** might or might not be considered homophones, depending upon the choice of pronunciation of **buoy**. Other difficulties involve the particular dictionary used for the suggested pronunciations. Lexicographers vary slightly in their choice of diacritical symbols used to represent particular sounds. The message from the above information is: Use these words as they fit the specific learning situation. Rule out those pairs of words which might be confusing to the learners involved. These bidialectal words, however, may be used for a class discussion regarding pronunciation choices.*

*The sets of words below appear only once (in alphabetical order) unless the initial letters of any word in the set differ. In such a case, as in **cell** and **sell**, the sets appear under each of the beginning letters. The pairs of words are listed according to the first possible alphabetical arrangement. The majority of proper words were omitted, although a few frequently used ones were included. Additional pairs of homophones may be formed by adding inflections of some of the included sets. For example, **beats** and **beets** could also be considered homophones. Only a few inflected forms are included in this list.*

*A wide range of difficulty is inherent in these sets of homophones. Some sets, such as **be** and **bee**, are easier to learn and understand in earlier grades than are words such as **descension** and **dissension**. Again, the instructor may choose not to include any which may not fit the educational needs of the learner.*

accidence, accidents	awful, offal	berry, bury	but, butt	chic, sheik
acts, axe, ax	axel, axil, axle	berth, birth	cache, cash	Chile, chili, chilly
ad, add	axes, axis	better, bettor	Cain, cane	choir, quire
adds, ads, adz, adze	aye, eye, I	bight, bite	cannon, canon	choler, collar
adherence, adherents	babble, Babel	billed, build	can't, cant	choral, coral
adieu, ado	bade, bayed	bird, burred	canter, cantor	chorale, corral
adolescence,	bail, bale	blew, blue	canvas, canvass	chord, cord, cored
adolescents	bait, bate	bloc, block	capital, Capitol	chute, shoot
aid, aide	baize, bays	boar, bore	carat, karat, caret,	cinque, sink, sync
ail, ale	bald, bawled, balled	board, bored	carrot	cion, scion, Sion
air, heir, ere, e'er	balks, box	boarder, border	carol, Carroll	cist, cyst
aisle, isle, I'll	ball, bawl	bode, bowed	cast, caste	cite, site, sight
ait, ate, eight	balm, bomb	bold, bowled	caudal, caudle	clack, claque
all, awl	band, banned	bolder, boulder	cause, caws	Claus, clause, claws
allowed, aloud	banns, bans	bole, boll, bowl	cedar, ceder, seeder	cleek, clique
all ready, already	bard, barred	boos, booze	cede, seed	clew, clue
all together, altogether	bare, bear	born, borne, bourn,	ceil, seal, seel	climb, clime
all ways, always	bark, barque	bourne	ceiling, sealing,	close, clothes
altar, alter	baron, barren	borough, burrow,	seeling	coal, cole, kohl
analyst, annalist	baroness, barrenness	burro	cell, sell	coaled, cold
an, Ann	base, bass	bough, bow	cellar, seller	coarse, course
ant, aunt	based, baste	boy, buoy	cense, cents, scents,	coat, cote
antecedence,	bask, basque, Basque	brae, bray	sense, since	coax, cokes
antecedents	bay, bey	braid, brayed	censer, censor	colonel, kernel
arc, ark	be, bee	braise, braze, brays	cent, sent, scent	color, culler
ascent, assent	beach, beech	brake, break	cerate, serrate	complement,
asperate, aspirate	beadle, beetle	brewed, brood	cere, sear, seer, sere	compliment
asperation, aspiration	beal, bill	brews, bruise	cereal, serial	con, khan
assistance, assistants	beat, beet	briar, brier	cession, session	confidant, confident
attendance, attendants	beau, bow	bridal, bridle	chance, chants	consequence,
aural, oral	been, bin, Ben	Britain, Briton	chard, charred	consequents
auricle, oracle	beer, bier	broom, brume	check, Czech	consonance,
away, aweigh	berg, burg	brows, browse	chews, choose	consonants

GA1304

coo, coup
coolly, coolie
core, corps
correspondence, correspondents
council, counsel
coward, cowered
crewel, cruel
cue, queue
currant, current
cymbal, symbol
days, daze
dear, deer
den, din
dense, dents
dental, dentil
dependence, dependents
descension, dissension
descent, dissent
desert, dessert
dew, do, due
done, dun
draft, draught
droop, drupe
dual, duel
dyeing, dying
earn, ern, erne, urn
earnest, Ernest
eau, oh, owe
eave, eve, Eve
eek, eke
e'er, ere, air, heir
eight, ate, ait
elicit, illicit
elusion, illusion
emerge, immerge
emersion, immersion
eminent, imminent
eruption, irruption
ewe, yew, you
ewer, you're, your
ewes, use, yews
exercise, exorcise
expedience, expedients
eye, I, aye
eyelet, islet
fade, fayed
fain, fane, feign
faint, feint
fair, fare
fairy, ferry
falter, faulter
faun, fawn
faze, phase
feat, feet
fiancé, fiancée
filter, philter
find, fined

finds, fines
fir, fur
fisher, fissure
flair, flare
flea, flee
flecks, flex
flew, flue, flu
Flo, floe, flow
flocks, phlox
flour, flower
foaled, fold
for, fore, four
foreword, forward
forth, fourth
foul, fowl
franc, frank, Frank
frays, phrase
frees, freeze, frieze
friar, fryer
froes, froze
furs, furze
gage, gauge
gait, gate
gall, Gaul
gamble, gambol
gem, gym
genes, jeans
gest, jest
gild, guild
gilt, guilt
gin, jinn
glair, glare
glows, gloze
gnawed, nod
gneiss, nice
gnome, nome, Nome
gnu, new, knew
gored, gourd
graft, graphed
grate, great
grater, greater
gray, grey
grays, graze
grease, Greece
grew, grue
guessed, guest
guide, guyed
hail, hale
hair, hare
hairy, Harry
hall, haul
halve, have
handmade, handmaid
hangar, hanger
hart, heart
hay, hey
hays, haze
heal, heel, he'll
hear, here
heard, herd

he'd, heed
heir, air, ere, e'er
hem, him, hymn
heroin, heroine
hew, hue, Hugh
higher, hire
ho, hoe
hoard, horde
hoarse, horse
hoes, hose
hold, holed
hole, whole
holey, holy, wholly
hostel, hostile
hour, our
I, eye, aye
idle, idol, idyl, idyll
I'll, aisle, isle
illicit, elicit
illusion, elusion
immerge, emerge
immersion, emersion
imminent, eminent
in, inn
incidence, incidents
innocence, innocents
instance, instants
intense, intents
irruption, eruption
islet, eyelet
its, it's
jeans, genes
jest, gest
jinn, gin
karat, carat, caret, carrot
Ken, kin
kernel, colonel
key, quay
khan, con
kill, kiln
kissed, kist
knap, nap
knave, nave
knead, need, kneed
kneel, neal
knew, gnu, new
knight, night
knit, nit
knob, nob
knot, not
know, no
knows, nose, noes
lac, lack
lacks, lax
lade, laid
lain, lane
lase, lays, laze
lay, lei
leach, leech

lead, led
leaf, lief, Lief
leak, leek
lean, lien
leased, least
lends, lens
lessen, lesson
levee, levy
lewd, looed
liar, lyre
lichen, liken
licker, liquor
lie, lye
lieu, loo
light, lite
lightening, lightning
lime, lyme
line, lion
links, linx
lo, low
load, lode, lowed
loan, lone
loch, lock
locks, lox
loon, lune
loot, lute
lumbar, lumber
made, maid
mail, male
main, Maine, mane
maize, maze
mall, maul
manner, manor
mantel, mantle
many, mini
marc, Mark, mark, marque
mare, mayor
marry, Mary, merry
marshal, martial
marten, martin
massed, mast
me, mi
mean, mien
meant, mint
meat, meet, mete
medal, meddle
meddler, medlar
meeting, meting
mewl, mule
mews, Muse, muse
might, mite
mil, mill
mina, myna
mince, mints
minor, miner
missal, missel, missile
missed, mist
moan, mown
moat, mote

mode, mowed
mood, mooed
moose, mousse
more, mower
morn, mourn
morning, mourning
mucous, mucus
muscle, mussel
mussed, must
mustard, mustered
nap, knap
naval, navel
nave, knave
nay, neigh
neal, kneel
necklace, neckless
need, knead, kneed
new, gnu, knew
niche, nick
night, knight
nit, knit
no, know
nob, knob
nod, gnawed
noes, knows, nose
Nome, gnome, nome
none, nun
not, knot
oak, oke
oar, o'er, or, ore
ode, ode, owed
offal, awful
oh, owe, eau
oleo, olio
one, won
oracle, auricle
oral, aural
our, hour
pa, paw
pac, pack
paced, paste
packed, pact
pair, pear, pare
palate, palette, pallet, pallette
passed, past
paten, patten
patience, patients
pause, paws
peace, piece
peak, peek, pique
peal, peel
pealed, peeled
pearl, purl
pedal, peddle
peer, pier
pen, pin
penance, pennants
pencil, pensile
pend, penned

pendant, pendent
per, purr
phase, faze
philter, filter
phlox, flocks
phrase, frays
pi, pie
pica, pika
picks, pyx
pistil, pistol
plain, plane
pleas, please
pliers, plyers
polar, poler
pole, poll
populace, populous
pore, pour
poring, pouring
praise, prase, prays, preys
pray, prey
precedence, precedents
presence, presents
pride, pried
prier, prior
pries, prize
prince, prints
principal, principle
profit, prophet
prophecy, prophesy
pros, prose
quay, key
quire, choir
queue, cue
rack, wrack
racks, rax
radical, radicle
raid, rayed
rail, rale
rain, reign, rein
raise, rays, raze
raised, rased, razed
raiser, razor
rancor, ranker
rap, wrap
rapped, rapt, wrapped
rapping, wrapping
ray, re
read, reed
read, red
real, reel
reave, reeve

recede, reseed
receipt, reseat
reck, wreck
repeal, repeel
rescind, resend
residence, residents
rest, wrest
retch, wretch
review, revue
rhyme, rime
right, rite, write
ring, wring
road, rode, rowed
roc, rock
roe, row
roes, rose, rows
role, roll
roles, rolls
rood, rude, rued
roomer, rumor
root, route
rote, wrote
rough, ruff
rouse, rows
rye, wry
sac, sack, sacque
sail, cell
sailer, sailor
sale, sell
sane, seine
scene, seen
scent, cent, sent
scents, cents, cense, sense, since
scion, cion, Sion
scull, skull
sea, see
seal, ceil, seel
sealing, ceiling, seeling
seam, seem
seamed, seemed
sear, cere, seer, sere
seas, sees, seize
seed, cede
seeder, cedar, ceder
sell, cell
seller, cellar
sequence, sequents
serf, surf
serge, surge
serial, cereal
serrate, cerate

session, cession
sew, so, sow
sewer, sower
sewer, suer
shear, sheer
sheik, chic
shier, shire, shyer
shone, shown
shoo, shoe
shoot, chute
sic, sick
side, sighed
sigher, sire
sighs, size
sight, cite, site
sign, sine, syne
sink, cinque, sync
slay, sleigh
slaying, sleighing
sleight, slight
sloe, slow
soar, sore
soared, sword
socks, sox
sol, sole, soul
sold, soled
some, sum
son, sun
sou, Sioux, Sue, sue
spade, spayed
spinned, spend
staid, stayed
stair, stare
stake, steak
stationary, stationery
steal, steel
step, steppe
stile, style
stoop, stoup, stupe
straight, strait
straighten, straiten
subtle, suttle, subtile
succor, sucker
suede, swayed
suite, sweet
sundae, Sunday
superintendence, superintendents
symbol, cymbal
tacked, tact
tacks, tax
tail, tale
talc, talk

tare, tear
taught, taut
tea, tee
team, teem
tear, tier
tears, tiers
ten, tin
tenants, tenents
tense, tents
tern, terne, turn
the, thee
their, there, they're
threw, through
throe, throw
throne, thrown
thyme, time
tide, tied
tier, tire, tyre
to, too, two
toad, toed, towed
tocsin, toxin
told, tolled
tole, toll
ton, tun
tongue, tung
toon, tune
tooter, tutor
tracked, tract
tray, trey
trussed, trust
unceded, unseeded
undo, undue
urn, earn, ern, erne
use, ewes, yews
vail, veil, vale
vain, vane, vein
vales, veils
vary, very
versed, verst
vial, vile, viol
vice, vise
wacks, wacs, wax, whacks
wade, weighed
wail, wale, whale
wain, wane
waist, waste
wait, weight
waits, weights
waive, wave
waiver, waver
want, wont, won't
war, wore

ward, warred
ware, wear
wares, wears
warn, worn
wart, wort
watt, wot, what
way, weigh
we, wee
weak, week
weal, we'll
weald, wield
weather, wether, whether
weave, we've
we'd, weed
weir, we're
weld, welled
wench, winch
which, wich, witch
whine, wine
whither, wither
whoa, woe
whole, hole
wholly, holey, holy
whoop, hoop
who's, whose
wind, wined
won, one
wood, would
worst, wurst
wrack, rack
wrap, rap
wrapped, rapped, rapt
wrapping, rapping
wreck, reck
wrest, rest
wretch, retch
wring, ring
wright, right, rite, write
wrote, rote
wrung, rung
wry, rye
yawn, yon
yew, you, ewe
yews, use, ewes
yoke, yolk
you'll, Yule
your, you're, ewer

GA1304

ANSWERS

Answers for Word Twisters

1. into, 2. cowboy, 3. hummingbird, 4. pigtail, 5. toenail, 6. before, 7. sees, seas, or seize, 8. half brother, 9. charley horse, 10. watchdog, 11. friendship, 12. ease, 13. sixty, 14. reindeer, 15. pigpen, 16. chairman, 17. belong, 18. bulldozer, 19. easy, 20. seesaw, 21. enlist, 22. footnote, 23. use, yews, or ewes, 24. bullfrog, 25. ringworm, 26. empty, 27. dogwood, 28. illegal, 29. honeymoon, 30. icy, 31. swordfish, 32. catfish, 33. bulldog, 34. rainbow, 35. tease, 36. dragnet, 37. seasick, 38. entire, 39. forerunners, 40. bellboy, 41. tennis, 42. sweepstakes, 43. wise, 44. pantry, 45. sleeping quarters, 46. pigeonhole, 47. exchange, 48. teepee, 49. rampage, 50. polecat, 51. housefly, 52. envy, 53. forearms, 54. encircle, 55. walking stick, 56. adverbs, 57. capsize, 58. heartburn, 59. horseradish, 60. deadlock, 61. essay, 62. entry, 63. dormouse, 64. deadpan, 65. inquire, 66. nightmare, 67. engineers, 68. butterfly, 69. foreign, 70. impair, 71. pipeline, 72. paradise, 73. excess, 74. countryside, 75. cashiers, 76. melancholy, 77. snapdragon, 78. dandelion, 79. canine, 80. canopies, 81. crocheted

Answers for Zany Antonyms

Menu, Womenu; Boise, Girlsie; Hurricane, Himicane or Hisicane;
Boycott, Girlcott; Mandate, Womandate

Answers for Who's Afraid of Phobophobiacs?

1. Vaccinophobiac, 2. Zoophobiac, 3. Thermophobiac,
4. Bibliophobiac, 5. Claustrophobiac, 6. Meteorophobiac

Answers for Eponyms for Vocabulary Fun

Scrooge, (L)leotard(s), (M)melba, Frisbee®

Answers for Those Crazy Idioms

1. A, 2. B, 3. B, 4. A, 5. B, 6. A. 7. A, 8. B. 9. B. 10. B, 11. B

CONTAINERS

Several activities in this book are groups of small cards. These cards may be stored in containers made of heavy paper. The patterns on the following two pages may be used for this purpose. Prepare as you wish, or follow the directions provided on page 143.

Use the patterns on this page and the following page as guides to prepare containers for the indicated activities. The following six steps are suggested:

1. Cut each shape from six-ply poster paper. Using a razor blade or a sharp instrument, crease at the dotted lines. Fold and use enough tape to hold in a box shape.

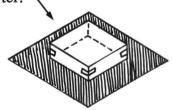

2. Cut a piece of self-adhesive decorative paper approximately two inches longer and wider than the original pattern. Peel the backing from the paper and place the taped box in the center.

3. Cut the adhesive paper as shown. Discard the unneeded sections.

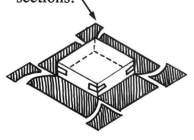

VOCABULARY RIDDLES

WORD TWISTER CARDS

*Cut two of this pattern for use with both **Worbic** and **Word Twister Cards**.*

*If box **lids** are desired, make your own guide from the provided base pattern by increasing the width and length each by an eighth of an inch.*

WORBIC CARDS

(Continued on the next page.)

GA1304

4. Push the curved pieces up the sides of the box and tuck the excess decorative cover inside.

TRIPLE TROUBLE CARDS

$\updownarrow$ *Extra space in pattern* $\updownarrow$

5. Push the remaining pieces up the sides and tuck the excess inside.

VOCABULARY VIVACITY CARDS

Special Note: *The depths of the containers on these pages are designed to accommodate cards copied onto paper commonly called index stock. Varying thicknesses exist for this type of paper. Also, the thickness of the complete set of cards will increase if laminating film or a clear self-adhesive covering is added to protect the cards. In those cases a deeper container will need to be prepared. To do this, cut a photocopy of the box pattern through the center and add the extra depth needed.*

6. If desired, paste the title on the side of the box. Insert the activity cards.

TRIPLE TROUBLE CARD 1
OPPOSITES: Give the opposite of each of the following words.

TRIPLE TROUBLE CARDS

GA1304